SUCCESS STARTS HERE

Purpose and Personal Initiative

EARL NIGHTINGALE

© Copyright 2019 – Nightingale Conant Corporation

All rights reserved. This book is protected by the copyright laws of the United States of America. No part of this publication may be reproduced, stored in or introduced into a retrieval system, or transmitted, in any form or by any means (electronic, mechanical, photocopying, recording or otherwise), without the prior written permission of the publisher. For permissions requests, contact the publisher, addressed "Attention: Permissions Coordinator," at the address below.

Published and Distributed by
SOUND WISDOM
PO Box 310
Shippensburg, PA 17257-0310
717-530-2122
info@soundwisdom.com
www.soundwisdom.com

While efforts have been made to verify information contained in this publication, neither the author nor the publisher assumes any responsibility for errors, inaccuracies, or omissions. While this publication is chock-full of useful, practical information, it is not intended to be legal or accounting advice. All readers are advised to seek competent lawyers and accountants to follow laws and regulations that may apply to specific situations. The reader of this publication assumes responsibility for the use of the information. The author and publisher assume no responsibility or liability whatsoever on the behalf of the reader of this publication.

The scanning, uploading and distribution of this publication via the Internet or via any other means without the permission of the publisher is illegal and punishable by law. Please purchase only authorized editions and do not participate in or encourage piracy of copyrightable materials.

Cover design by Eileen Rockwell

ISBN 13 TP: 978-1-64095-084-9

ISBN 13 eBook: 978-1-64095-085-6

Originally part of Nightingale Success program.

For Worldwide Distribution, Printed in the U.S.A.

1 2 3 4 5 6 / 21 20 19

Table of Contents

	Preface................................... 5
Foreword	by W. Clement Stone 9
Chapter One	Succeeding in Life with Goal-Setting 13
Chapter Two	Participating in Your Personal Evolution 35
Chapter Three	Making the Most of Opportunities 51
Chapter Four	Treading the Path to Success 65
Chapter Five	What You Need to Know to Succeed....... 83
Chapter Six	Finding Happiness in Life.................. 97
Chapter Seven	The Practice of Being Human.............. 115
Chapter Eight	Some of Life's Lessons 123
Chapter Nine	Thoughts on Existence.................... 133
	Earl Nightingale's Biography 157

Preface

Having spent a lifetime studying the factors that distinguish the world's top achievers from the rest of the population, Earl Nightingale understood the formula for success and dedicated his life to sharing this knowledge with the public through his radio broadcasts and audio programs. For Nightingale, this formula was remarkably simple: live a life of purpose, never losing interest in your pursuits and always working to better educate yourself, to remain open, and to operate from a position of gratitude and respect—respect for yourself, for others, and for the earth.

His message about finding and then living out your calling is one that every human being needs to hear, because he emphasizes that it is never too late to make the changes you need to realize your dreams. As he reiterates throughout his broadcasts, our time on earth is short; therefore, it is crucial that we spend every day in pursuit of the goals we have for ourselves, regardless of how distant or impossible they seem. Identify what gives you purpose, outline the steps you need to fulfill this purpose, then tackle them one at a time, never losing sight of what it is that you're after. In this way, you will become a self-actualized individual, living life with your "roots," as he says, "deep in a great, moving current—a moving stream of conscious direction—that will keep [you] on course, sailing steadily toward the destination [you] have chosen."

According to Nightingale, everyone, regardless of age, needs a goal to pursue in order to retain vitality and find true happiness. If you are in middle age, or retired, or ripe in years and think that a book on finding purpose in life is not relevant to you because your time has "passed," then you especially need to read the commentaries contained in this volume. As you'll discover, the only time it's too late to start living out your dreams is when you're dead, which is why Nightingale underscores the importance of not wasting one more day holding yourself back from the life you want to be living simply because of fear, habit, or worse—indifference.

Your Success Starts Here derives from *The Essence of Success*, a collection of over one hundred of Nightingale's original audio scripts published in 1993 by Nightingale-Conant Corporation. As W. Clement Stone notes in his original foreword, excerpted below, these scripts "have been extracted from the firm's archives and gathered from the private collections of many individuals who have contributed rare tapes and transcriptions to this tribute to one of the great motivational speakers and writers of this century."

Stone further explains: "Nightingale's radio colleague, Stephen D. King, whom Nightingale-Conant selected to narrate the audio

Preface

version of *The Essence of Success*, recalls that the project began as a simple, heartfelt memorial to a broadcasting great, whose career spanned more than four decades. 'Earl's friends and colleagues began assembling a cross-section of his 40-year output. They took snippets of his tapes, found transcriptions of his early broadcasts, and delved into several hours of never-before-heard tapes of interviews he gave. Soon the project took on a life of its own,' King recalled. 'The more they collected, the more they wanted to collect. Radio old-timers, hearing about the project, contributed rare tapes and transcriptions.' What they assembled has gone on to become far more than a memorial."

Now, those messages in *The Essence of Success* pertaining to finding purpose and taking the personal initiative necessary to live a successful, fulfilling life have been edited and re-collected in this power-packed volume. The chapters selected are those that will most directly guide you toward becoming self-actualized and amassing wealth—wealth in income, wealth in love and friendship, and wealth in personal satisfaction and happiness. If you've been afraid to venture out on a new path, need renewed inspiration to master the course you're already on, or simply want to learn how to live more mindfully and gratefully, *Your Success Starts Here* will provide you with the concrete tools you need to reach your personal goals.

In this volume, Nightingale says of a Sanskrit allegory: "It is as modern and important today as it was the day it first flashed across the mind of some person whose name has been long forgotten. And it will be just as important to thinking men and women 4,500 years from today, for real truth is as ageless as the mountains, as enduring as the sea." Nightingale's name is far from being forgotten, but this insight holds true for his messages: although produced decades ago, they contain real, ageless truths that will never lose relevance. *Your*

Success Starts Here invites you to begin the journey toward becoming your best self—the self whose dreams have become reality, whose relationships are flourishing, whose purpose is evident from the joy it derives from the minutiae of life, and whose legacy will extend beyond a narrow scope. As Nightingale notes, "success—beyond anything we might now imagine—lies in wait for those who can put together enough courage to actually live the life they imagine."

Foreword

A candle is not diminished by giving another candle light.

—Earl Nightingale

I FIRST MET EARL NIGHTINGALE more than four decades ago. Napoleon Hill and I had just begun an association which was to last ten years and carry us around the globe spreading the message that every individual could achieve lasting success by following a set of established principles that Hill had first written about in his all-time bestseller, *Think and Grow Rich*. Nightingale, at the time, had his own radio program on WGN in Chicago.

Dr. Hill and I had been discussing ways to promote his new book, *How to Raise Your Own Salary*, when Nightingale paid us a visit. "Your book *Think and Grow Rich* completely changed my life," he said. "I believe I knew all the principles before I read the book. But in *Think and Grow Rich,* they were in crystallized form. I could see them clearly. I decided to employ them—specifically, to double my earnings within a period of two weeks. I wrote my definite objective on a piece of paper and my earnings doubled in two weeks. I felt this might have been a coincidence. So I again decided to double my earnings and set a specific date. When I achieved this objective before the date set, I said to myself, 'This is no coincidence. Here I have a formula for success.'"

He looked at Napoleon Hill and continued: "I want to show my gratitude to you for *Think and Grow Rich*. I am here to help you all I can in any way."

Nightingale amazed me with the offer that followed. He would publicize *How to Raise Your Own Salary* at no cost to us. We decided to try him out to see if he was sincere. He was, and he did a magnificent job of publicizing the book. Sales were coming in volume.

Before the week was over, I called Nightingale, complimented him, and said, "I don't want something for nothing. We will pay you your regular rate beginning with your second week of broadcasting for us." Through Nightingale's efforts, we sold more copies of *How to Raise Your Own Salary* than through all other advertising and promotional media combined.

Nightingale and I and Napoleon Hill became great friends and we met often to discuss our common love of helping others learn to apply the principles of success in their own lives. It was one of the greatest experiences of my life to work with these outstanding individuals who were dedicated to the achievement of such noble objectives and to helping each other reach our own personal goals. It was at one of those meetings that I suggested to Nightingale that he reach out to hundreds of thousands more people than he was already reaching by multiplying himself.

Nightingale did multiply himself with the same intensity that he applied to reaching every goal he set for himself. He formed a partnership with Lloyd Conant to establish Nightingale-Conant to produce motivational recordings and special courses for listeners around the world. Their company literally pioneered the development, production, design, and marketing of motivational programs.

Nightingale-Conant was itself built upon fundamental principles of success. Their partnership was what I call a Mastermind Alliance, in which they worked together in a spirit of perfect harmony, toward a common purpose. Each had skills that complemented the other's. Conant was the business and marketing brain, and Nightingale was the company's spokesperson. Conant ran the operation and Nightingale chaired the board of directors. Together they made the company highly successful.

They had one goal: to publish the best recorded self-help material available anywhere. Though they have both passed away, the Nightingale-Conant legacy is a company built upon principles, values, and ethics so strong that it survives them, and the organization that bears their names has set the standard for and become synonymous with quality in motivational recordings.

Earl Nightingale was in many ways a "river person," a term he often used to describe other great men. River people, he believed, recognize their life's purpose early on. "They are born to spend their lives in great rivers of the most absorbing interest, and they throw themselves into those rivers wholly," he said. He used Wolfgang Amadeus Mozart and Leonardo da Vinci as examples of river people.

Nightingale's destiny, the river that swept him to great heights, was to convey the principles of success to millions of listeners in a style that was uniquely his own. No one who ever heard his distinctive gravelly voice as he recounted his own brand of insightful inspiration or read the wise words that flowed from his pen will ever forget Earl Nightingale. His profound thoughts touched and changed the lives of millions.

Nightingale believed that we are not all born river people. It takes some of us longer to find our river—our own specific, individual purpose in life. We must somehow set about discovering what it is within ourselves, Nightingale wrote, "with the patience and assiduity of a paleontologist on an important dig."

The stories included in this book may hold the key to helping you better understand yourself as you attempt to find your own river. You will know you have found it when your purpose in life demands fulfillment just as Nightingale's mission to carry his inspirational message of success to others led him to multiply himself a thousandfold through writing and recording and through his partnership with Lloyd Conant. Your river will become your burning desire in life and it will fill you with energy and enthusiasm.

Though Earl Nightingale's brief candle flickered and was forever extinguished on March 25, 1989, it continues to light the candles of others. His works stand as a beacon of hope. His writings and recordings shine as brightly today as they did when they were first created. They are yours to read and enjoy, and to help light the way in your own life.

—W. Clement Stone

Chapter One

Succeeding in Life with Goal-Setting

The Strangest Secret

WHY DO PEOPLE with goals succeed in life...and people without them fail? Well, let me tell you something, which, if you really understand it, will alter your life immediately. You'll suddenly find that good luck just seems to be attracted to you. The things you want will just seem to fall in line. And from now on, you won't have the problems, the worries, the gnawing lump of anxiety that perhaps you've experienced before. Doubt, fear...well, they'll be things of the past.

Here's the key to success and the key to failure: we become what we think about. Now, read that again: we become what we think about.

Throughout all history, the great wise men, teachers, philosophers, and prophets have disagreed with one another on many different things. It is only on this one point that they are in complete and unanimous agreement.

Marcus Aurelius, the great Roman emperor, said: "A man's life is what his thoughts make of it."

Benjamin Disraeli said, "Everything comes if a man will only wait. I have brought myself by long meditation to the conviction that a human being with a settled purpose must accomplish it and that nothing can resist a will that will stake even existence for its fulfillment."

Ralph Waldo Emerson said, "A man is what he thinks about all day long."

In the Bible, Mark 9:23 reads: "If thou canst believe, all things are possible to him that believeth."

My old friend, Dr. Norman Vincent Peale, put it this way: "This is one of the greatest laws in the universe. Fervently do I wish I had discovered it as a very young man. The great law briefly and simply stated that if you think in negative terms you will get negative results. If you think in positive terms you will achieve positive results. That is the simple fact," he went on to say, "which is the basis of an astonishing law of prosperity and success. In three words: Believe and Succeed."

Well, it's pretty apparent, isn't it? And every person who discovered this (for a while) believed that he was the first one to work it out. We become what we think about.

Now, how does it work? Why do we become what we think about? Well, I'll tell you how it works, as far as we know. Now to do this, I want to tell you about a situation that parallels the human mind.

Suppose a farmer has some land, and it's good, fertile land. Now, the land gives the farmer a choice: he may plant in that land whatever he chooses. The land doesn't care. It's up to the farmer to make the decision.

Now remember, we're comparing the human mind to the land because the mind, like the land, doesn't care what you plant in it. It will return what you plant, but it doesn't care what you plant.

Now, let's say that the farmer has two seeds in his hand. One is a seed of corn; the other is nightshade, a deadly poison. He digs two little holes in the earth, and he plants both seeds—one corn, the other nightshade. He covers up the holes, waters and takes care of the land, and what will happen? Invariably, the land will return what is planted. As it's written in the Bible, "As ye sow, so shall ye reap."

Remember, the land doesn't care. It will return poison in just as wonderful abundance as it will corn. So up come the two plants— one corn, one poison.

The human mind is far more fertile, far more incredible and mysterious, than the land, but it works the same way. It doesn't care what we plant: success; failure; a concrete, worthwhile goal; or confusion, misunderstanding, fear, anxiety and so on. But what we plant, it must return to us.

You see, the human mind is the last great unexplored continent on earth. It contains riches beyond our wildest dreams. It will return anything we want to plant.

Now, you might say, "Well, if that's true, why don't people use their minds more?" Well, I think they've figured out an answer to that one, too. Our mind comes as standard equipment at birth. It's free. And things that are given to us for nothing we place little value on. Things that we pay money for we value.

The paradox is that exactly the reverse is true. Everything that's really worthwhile in life came to us free: our minds, our souls, our bodies, our hopes, our dreams, our ambitions, our intelligence, and our love of family, children, friends, and country. All these priceless possessions are free.

But the things that cost us money are actually very cheap and can be replaced at any time. A good man can be completely wiped out and make another fortune. He can do that several times. Even if our home burns down we can rebuild it. But the things we got for nothing we can never replace.

The human mind isn't used because we take it for granted. Familiarity breeds contempt. Our minds can do any kind of job we assign to them, but generally speaking we use them for little jobs instead of big, important ones. Universities have proven that most of us are operating on about 10 percent or less of our abilities.

So decide now: What is it you want? Plant your goal in your mind. It's the most important decision you'll ever make in your entire life.

You see, the very law that gives us success is a two-edged sword. We must control our thinking. The same rule that can lead a man to a life of success, wealth, happiness, and all the things he ever dreamed of for himself and his family—that very same law can lead him into the gutter. It's all in how he uses it—for good or for bad. This is the strangest secret in the world!

Sailing to a Port of Call

I HAD THE GOOD FORTUNE to be raised near a harbor on the sea. As a kid, I used to spend hours down on the docks, watching the ships loading and unloading. They'd bring in cargoes from the distant and romantic ports all over the world, and I used to stand there with a faraway look in my eyes, envying those sailors who were so fortunate to travel to all those places. They traveled over the distant horizon to places I could only imagine or read about in my geography books.

I hung around so much that some of the mates and skippers finally recognized me and actually invited me onboard. I guess you can imagine the heaven that was for me. They'd take me from the engine room to the forecastle and finally to the place I liked best— the navigation bridge. The bridge had the best view, but it was much more than that. It was there that the ship was controlled and steered into all those distant places I dreamed of. (Once I was even invited to lunch, and I didn't get over that for months!)

It's strange how something like that can have such an overwhelming fascination for a youngster and exert such an influence over his life. As soon as I was old enough, I was on a ship, and I sailed to quite a few of those distant, deep-water ports. No matter how long the trip, I never got tired of sailing and watching the sea in all its different moods. Entering a distant port, even if I'd been there before, was always a brand-new thrill.

Over the years, I've tried to figure out why I like ships so much. I believe I've come up with the answer. Ships operate the way people ought to, I believe, but so few do. Maybe you've never given it much thought, but at any given moment, a ship has a direction. That is, either she's sailing to a predetermined port of call, or she's in port, getting ready to sail to another one. You can climb up to the navigation bridge of a big, far-sailing ship and ask the captain where he's going. He can tell you instantly—and in one sentence.

How many people do you know who can do the same thing? It seems that most people want so many different things—or at least they think they want them—that they're unable to focus their efforts, their minds, their hearts on anything specific. And all this leads to is doubt and confusion. They're like the guy who jumped on a horse and rode off in all directions at once. They don't recognize how vital it is to pick one port that's important, then sail to it, rest and refit for a little while, and then sail to another port. In this way, in not so many years, a person can set and reach his goals one by one until finally he has a tremendous pile of accomplishments in which he can take pride. He has all the things he wants just because he had sense enough to realize he could do well only one thing at a time.

There's another analogy that fits here, and maybe it makes the most important point of all. If a ship tied to a dock for some reason had no place to go, she would stay there until she fell apart from rust and disuse. A ship's engine isn't started until she has some place to go. Here again, it's the same with people. This is why it's so important that each of us has a port of call we want to reach—a goal, a place to get to that we feel will be better than the place in which we now find ourselves. If we don't, why, we might never cast off. We might never start our engines and know the thrill of sailing a charted course to a place we can't see for fully 99 percent of the journey. But we know it's there, and we know that if we keep sailing toward it, we'll reach it.

If someone came up to you today and asked you what your next port of call is—that is, where you're going—could you answer him in one sentence, as could the captain on the bridge of his ship? If not, maybe you'd like to give it some thought.

Tips for Setting Goals

A CLINICAL ASSOCIATE professor of psychiatry, Dr. Ari Kiev, writes, "In my practice as a psychiatrist, I have found that helping people to develop personal goals has proven to be the most effective way to help them cope with problems. Observing the lives of people who have mastered adversity, I have noted," he writes, "that they have established goals and sought with all their effort to achieve them. From the moment they decided to concentrate all their energies on a specific objective, they began to surmount the most difficult odds."

So writes Dr. Kiev in his book *A Strategy for Daily Living*. He writes, "The establishment of a goal is the key to successful living. And the most important step toward achieving an objective is first to define it. I'm sure you have at least thirty minutes a day in which to list your thoughts about possible goals. Set aside such a period each day for a month. At the end of that time, choose from the possible objectives you have listed the one that seems most important, and record it separately on a single card. Carry this card with you at all times. Think about this objective every day. Create concrete mental images of the goal, as if you've already accomplished it."

The doctor points out, "You can determine your special talents or strengths in a number of ways, ranging from psychological tests to an analysis of the unexpressed wishes in your dreams. No one method works for everyone. You might start, for example, by clipping and posting newspaper articles that interest you. After thirty days, see if there isn't some trend suggestive of a deep-seated interest or natural inclination. Keep alert to the slightest indications of any special skills or talents, even when they seem silly or unimportant.

"From this exercise, you should be able to get some sense of potential strengths. Whenever you discover a strength or talent, think of five possible ways to develop it. Write these down on a card as well, and check them periodically to keep them fresh in your mind.

"Focus on one objective at a time. Like a servo-mechanism, the brain, set on a target, will call into play those mental processes that will bring your efforts to fruition. Your actions will conform to your expectations, thereby bringing about the event. If you believe that you will reach your objective, you will continue to work at a task until you have accomplished it."

And he suggests that we be aware of situations that generate the five great enemies of peace: avarice, ambition, envy, anger, and pride. Petrarch said, "If those enemies were to be banished, we should infallibly enjoy perpetual peace." Old advice—perennial advice—and perennially forgotten. It has been said that we need reminding as much as we need educating. Even Petrarch, in the fourteenth century, knew all about this subject.

Dr. Kiev got the idea of writing his book because of a young businessman who visited his office saying he needed a set of guidelines to follow that would let him function without professional help, in the face of considerable confusion and despair caused by serious personal problems.

So take the good advice of the psychiatrist, Dr. Ari Kiev. And don't be afraid of failure. As Herodotus wrote, "It is better by noble boldness to run the risk of being subject to half of the evils we anticipate than to remain in cowardly listlessness for fear of what may happen."

Finding Your Great Motivating Desire

The key that unlocks energy is desire. It's also the key to a long and interesting life. If we expect to create any drive, any real force within ourselves, we have to get excited.

DID YOU EVER WONDER where those human dynamos, those people who can pack as much work into one day as most of us do in two, get all the energy and drive that makes them go? Well, the source of drive and energy in human beings is known. It's the personal excitement that comes from a great motivating desire.

If you ask most people why they get out of bed in the morning and slug away all day on the job, they'll probably have to think about it awhile before coming up with an answer. When they do, it's usually along the line of "Oh, to pay the rent" or "To put food on the table." Answers like these aren't exciting. I belong to the group that thinks life is far too short to be dull. Shelter and food are things we need, but unless we're living out in the street or starving to death, we're not up to getting too excited about a place to sleep or something to eat.

Those who have no exciting reason for getting out of bed in the morning may be fine people, but they never seem to accomplish anything out of the ordinary, and they miss a lot of fun and a lot of rewards that they could be enjoying. They haven't got the drive to become outstanding because they don't have a great motivating desire.

The key that unlocks energy is desire. It's also the key to a long and interesting life. If we expect a person to do something we want him to do, we have to get him excited. And if we expect to create any drive, any real force within ourselves, we have to get excited. We have to decide on something we desire very much—a goal that fires our imagination with a mental picture of having something, doing something, or being something.

In a company I once surveyed, one of the men had won the admiration of all the others. I noticed that he had thorough knowledge of his company, its products, its markets, and its competitors. He took pains to understand his customers and their problems. These things, along with an easy manner and a good personality, marked him as an outstanding employee. We asked him about all this, and he said, "When I came to this company a few years back, I decided to shoot for a manager's job in one of our districts. I'm doing everything I can to be the kind of man who would have that job."

Well, that explained it. In his mind, he was already running his own district. The rest of him was merely carrying out the motions that would soon propel him into the job he wanted. Meanwhile, he was enjoying himself tremendously. The mental image of being a district manager so appealed to him that he found all the enthusiasm, energy, and drive he was going to need to achieve that position. Everything he said and did in his current job had to conform to the image he held in his mind. He was outstanding because nothing less than his best would fit with the goal he'd picked out.

Of course he'll get that district manager job and all that goes with it. People with unusual drive and energy, people who excel, are the ones who have given themselves a mental picture, a goal to work toward. And the amount of drive they possess will always be in exact proportion to the strength and desire to make that mental picture a reality, to reach that goal.

We don't have to worry about setting a goal we can never reach; that's the strange and wonderful thing about humans, something that most people seem to miss. We never seriously desire anything we can't possibly have. If you get all fired up over something, whether it's an executive position in your company or the income you feel you and your family need to do and have the things you want, if you can clearly envision how it will feel to satisfy your desire, well, then it can be yours.

Arnold Bennett wrote that the kind of desire that triggers drive and energy within us isn't some vague hankering, some undefined wish. The productive kind of desire is real, it's concrete, it's a mental picture that will never leave us alone. It's always there in front of our minds, prodding and poking, goading us on. It's an obsession, a whip. It has no mercy, and we'll never be satisfied until we've achieved that which we truly desire.

Well, how about you? What's your goal? What is it that gets you fired up every time you think about it? If you have such a goal, you'll never have to worry about the drive and energy you'll need to achieve it. But if you find that you lack drive, that you're short on energy, give it some thought. Decide on the dream that's more important to you than any other. Then begin to make that dream a reality. You can—and you'll find that you've got all the drive you need and all the energy you want.

Long-Range and Short-Range Goals

A MAN HUNTING TIGERS in India was suddenly surprised by a huge Bengal tiger—it was almost on top of him. The man raised his rifle and fired, but he overshot and missed. The tiger, frightened by the man and thrown off stride by the noise of the gun, leaped toward the hunter. But the leap was too wide, and he missed his prey.

The man returned to camp and spent several hours perfecting his aim for short distances and quick firing. On the following day, he again stalked the tiger. Finally, he spotted the beast at some distance. The tiger was practicing short leaps.

It's a charming little story, and it started me thinking about a subject it seems we can't say too much about—goals.

Did you ever sit down and make a list of everything you want? It's a very interesting experiment, and you'll make some surprising discoveries. You might find that you have already managed to get most of the things you have seriously wanted. Or if you don't have most or all of them, chances are you're now in the process of getting them.

If your list contains some items you want very much but don't have, you might ask yourself why you've failed to get them. Chances are that you haven't tried very hard. Or perhaps you felt, for one reason or another, that these things are completely beyond your ability to achieve. But on second look, they might make very worthwhile goals.

At any rate, it's a good idea to have two lists of things you want. The first list would include those bigger goals that relate to your career or the overall good of your life or your family. These might include the position and/or income you're working toward, perhaps a higher educational degree, a certain amount of money in your savings account, a plateau of business success, or that beautiful home you've had your eye on.

The other list could be a fun list. It might include the car you want for no good reason except it's the car you happen to want, rededicating the house, getting new furniture, traveling to some special place—perhaps abroad—buying a new wardrobe. This is a list of things you want just because you want them.

Now, here's where the story of the tiger comes in. We all should have long-range goals. These should be on our first list, and each of them should be numbered in the order of importance to us. These are goals that might take five years or longer to achieve. They're extremely worthwhile to us, and we should be working toward them daily. These are the goals that give meaning and direction and substance to our lives.

But we also need short-range goals. These are the goals that add zest and interest to our lives, and fun, and break up the monotony of the long haul for the long-range goals. We need to practice these short jumps, too.

If you're honest with yourself about the things you want—not idle, will-o'-the-wisp wishes that change from day to day but things you're serious about—you'll find that they all can be yours, and in a surprisingly short time, if they're taken one at a time.

It's been said that "people can have anything they want; the trouble is that they don't know what they want." Get off by yourself for a quiet hour or two, and make your two lists. It's fun and very rewarding.

What Happens When You Run Out of Goals

HERE ARE SOME INTERESTING QUESTIONS for you. You might want to try answering them. One: If you could completely change places with any other person in the world, would you do it? And who would that person be? Two: If you could work at any job you could choose, would that work be different from the work you're now doing? Three: If you could live in any part of the country you want to live in, would you move from where you're now living? Four: If you could go back to age twelve and live your life from that point over again, would you do it?

Studies indicate that the great majority of people, even though they have a certain amount of dissatisfaction with their present lives and don't seem to be as happy as they might be, will answer "no" to all four questions. What brought this to mind is an attorney friend of mine who confided that now that he's accomplished everything he's worked and struggled for so long to achieve, he finds himself depressed more and more of the time. He has a fine practice and an excellent income, a beautiful home, a wife and children to whom he's devoted. In fact, everything is finally just as he'd planned it for so many years. And for no reason that he can put his finger on, all the fun and enthusiasm have strangely disappeared. He's listless and unhappy, and he can't think of a single reason why.

This has become a common modern malady, and it's what so often happens when a person runs out of goals. This is when the game of life begins to go to pot, and the person needs to remind himself of the basic rules for successful, enthusiastic living. And the first rule is that a human being must have something worthwhile toward which he's working. Without that, everything else—even the most remarkable achievements of the past and all the trappings of worldly success—tend to turn sour. Achieving our life goals can be compared to opening our presents on Christmas morning and watching those we love open theirs. We look forward to the day, plan and work toward it. Suddenly it's there. All the presents have been opened, and then what?

Well, we must then turn our thoughts and attention to other things. The successful novelist begins planning his next book before he completes the one he's working on. The scientist always has something new and challenging to turn to when he completes a project. The teacher has a new class coming up. The young family has children to raise and get through school, the new home to buy, the promotion to work for.

But for millions who reach their forties and fifties and find they've done all they set out to do and that there are no new challenges to give them stimulus and direction, there often comes the most trying time of their lives—the search for meaning, for new meaning, and it must be found if the old interest and vitality are to be restored to their lives, if they're to achieve renewal as persons.

If they understand this, even the search for new meaning can bring new interest into their lives. They've got to say to themselves, "Alright, I've done what I've set out to do. Now I must find something new and interesting to do."

Getting back to our questions, the thought of going back to age twelve fills most people with a dread bordering on horror. They wouldn't do it for anything. And the upshot of the whole thing is that most people are living lives they themselves have fashioned and have or are getting what they really want, or at least what they're willing to settle for.

And when this is brought to their attention, they often begin to get a lot more enjoyment from the life they've got. They begin to enjoy themselves more and realize that things aren't so bad after all.

> **SUCCESS STARTS HERE**
>
> *Do you appreciate the life
> you have fashioned for yourself?*
>
> *When was the last time
> you assessed your long-term goals?*
>
> *Are you prepared to create new goals after
> you have accomplished your current goals?*

The River, or the Goal

IF YOU'RE GOING TO BE a big success as a human being, you have to fit into one of two groups or belong to both of them, it seems to me. So let's talk about these two groups of very successful men and women.

The first group belongs to what I call "the river." These are men and women who have found, often early in life although not always, a great river of interest into which they throw themselves with exuberance and abandon. They are quite happy to spend their lives working and playing in that river.

For some, the river may be a particular branch of science; for others, one of the arts. There are some physicians, for example, who are so wrapped up in medicine that they hate to leave it; even after a sixteen-hour day, they can't wait to get back to it. For others, quitting time comes as a welcome reward when they can indulge themselves in other interests.

There are some people who are happiest and most alive when they're in their river—in whatever business or career or profession it happens to be. And success comes to such people as inevitably as a sunrise. In fact, they are successes the moment they find their great field of interest; the worldly trappings of success will always come in time. Such people don't have to ask, "What will I do with my life?" Their work is a magnet for them, and they can't imagine doing anything else.

We all know such people…or about such people. Doing what they do is even more important to them than the rewards they earn for doing it. So much for the river people.

The second group of successful people are those who are goal-oriented. These people have not necessarily found a particular river and can be quite happy doing a number of things. It's the goals they set that are important to them, and they're quite aware that there are many roads that can lead to their goals.

Someone once said, "Americans can have anything they seriously make up their minds to have. The trouble is that most of them never make up their minds about anything." Goal-oriented people do make up their minds about what they want, and they keep their eyes and their enthusiasm on the goal they've established until it becomes a reality in their lives. Then they set a new goal, if they're wise.

One of the problems with this latter group is that after achieving a number of goals and becoming quite successful, they can run out of goals and become listless and unhappy. But not the river people. Their interest in what they're doing never fades.

So if you're going to be a big success, chances are you need to be a river person or a goal-oriented person, or both—the two groups, you see, are not mutually exclusive.

It's Not the Destination

So the person who knows what he wants knows what he must become, and he then fixes his attention on the preparation and development of himself.

I READ THE GREAT GREEK POEM by Constantine Cavafy titled *Ithaka,* and in it we're reminded that it is the voyage and the adventures on the way that count, not the arrival itself. Cervantes said the same thing.

This seems to be a most difficult truth to understand. This is not to say that a person's goal in life is unimportant. On the contrary, it's vital. For without a goal, a distant destination, we would not begin the trip at all. Instead, we'd run around in circles, endlessly following the shoreline around and around our tiny island. Every person needs a great and distant goal toward which to strive. But in traveling toward it, he should try to keep in mind that the fabled land he seeks has shores much like the one he left behind, that its purpose is not so much a resting place but, rather, the reason for the trip.

Where a person goes is not nearly as important as how he gets there. That a house is built is not all that important. It is the manner in which it is built that makes it great, average, or poor. That we live is not nearly as important as the manner in which we live.

I think that it's misunderstanding this that often keeps people in a state of unhappiness and anxiety. They forget to enjoy the trip. They forget what they're really looking for, or what they should be looking for—the discovery of themselves. This is the island toward which everyone should journey. It's a difficult journey, beset, like the travels of Ulysses, with many dangers and hardships. But it gives real meaning to life, and there are many rich rewards to be found along the way—all kinds of serendipitous benefits.

It means asking the questions that are hard to answer: Where am I going? Why am I going there? What do I really want, and why do I want it? Am I gradually realizing my potential? Am I discovering my best talents and abilities and using them to their fullest? Am I living fully extended in my one chance at life on earth? Am I really living? Who am I?

These are the questions that all people must ask themselves and answer. As Emerson said, "Though we travel the world over to find the beautiful, we must carry it with us, or we find it not."

Whatever you're looking for must first be found within you, whether it be peace, happiness, riches, or great accomplishments. Everything we do outwardly is only an expression of what we are inwardly. To ask for anything else is as absurd as looking for apples on an oak tree.

So the person who knows what he wants knows what he must become, and he then fixes his attention on the preparation and development of himself. As he grows toward the ideal he holds in his mind, he finds interest, zest, and joy on the journey. He looks forward to tomorrow, but he also enjoys today, for it is the tomorrow he looked forward to yesterday. He knows that if he cannot find meaning and value in his present, he will very likely be missing it in his future. Today is the future of five years ago. Are you enjoying it as much as you thought you would? Have you progressed to the point you wanted then to reach?

These are the questions that make us think.

Chapter Two

Participating in Your Personal Evolution

Wiping Away Negativity

The mature person strives for strength—strength of purpose, strength of mind, and strength of character. Only these can give us peace and serenity, joy and accomplishment.

I REMEMBER AS A CHILD in school watching my teacher write the word *ain't* on the blackboard. Then she had all of us look at the word for a long time. Finally, very slowly, she erased it. As she did, she told us to erase it from our minds, never to use it again. As the word disappeared from the blackboard, it disappeared from our minds. I've never forgotten the incident and how effective it was.

From time to time, we all need to clean the slate of our lives—to face up to and then wipe away certain emotions and unrewarding habits of thinking and behavior that hold us back. Some of these things that need to be wiped away can sour and spoil our lives and rob us of the success we seek.

I read a story once about a man who decided to do something about an enormous piece of granite that rose up out of the ground near his house. He got a chisel and a hammer, and before long he had carved an excellent reproduction of an elephant. His neighbor and passersby were amazed because it looked for all the world like a real elephant grazing in his yard.

A friend asked the amateur sculptor how he ever managed to reproduce so faithfully the form of an elephant without a model to go by. The man replied, "I just chipped away everything that didn't look like an elephant."

For a person to build a rich and rewarding life for himself, there are certain qualities and bits of knowledge that he needs to acquire. But there are also things—harmful attitudes, superstitions, emotions—that he needs to chip away. A person needs to chip away everything that doesn't look like the person he or she most wants to become.

The mature person strives for strength—strength of purpose, strength of mind, and strength of character. Only these can give us peace and serenity, joy and accomplishment.

In cutting things away, an excellent place to begin is with animosity toward others. Getting rid of hatred and animosity is like putting down a hundred-pound weight. We may hurt no one else by hating, but we do serious damage to ourselves. It shows in the face, in the attitude, and in the person's life. Ulcers, high blood pressure, colitis, and heart disease are physical ailments that can often be traced to hate and even minor resentments. Beyond that, these harmful emotions can strangle a person's creative ability and will to win.

It is the unfailing mark of the little person—the person who has failed to grow—to spend his life dreaming and plotting about "getting even" for real or fancied injuries. History shows that a person who wants revenge brings it only upon himself.

Lincoln was famous for not holding a grudge. He put his political enemies, Stanton, Seward, and Chase, into his presidential cabinet.

Benjamin Disraeli, England's brilliant prime minister, did favors for many who bitterly opposed him. He said, "I never trouble to be avenged. When a man injures me, I put his name on a slip of paper and lock it up in a drawer. It is marvelous to see how the men I have so labeled have a knack of disappearing."

In cleaning the slate of our lives, we should do all in our power to get rid of hate, self-pity, guilt, and remorse. All that we have is the present moment and the future. They can be anything we want them to be.

We Invent Ourselves

HAVE YOU GIVEN MUCH THOUGHT to the fact that you create yourself? You do, to an altogether unsuspected extent, simply by the choices you make—by the things you decide to do... or decide not to do.

As Kierkegaard said, "The self is only that which it is in the process of becoming." So it is that an adult can stand in front of a full-length mirror and take a good look at what he's created.

We leave home, and we form ourselves into new people; and we learn, as Thomas Wolfe learned, that we can't go home again, that we don't fit as well as we used to. We wonder, after a visit, as we leave to regain our lives, what happened; if something is wrong, what the strangeness was. It is simply that we are different now, and going back home again is like trying to get a two-year-old shoe on a teenager. It's not going to fit anymore.

We have shaped ourselves into new people. And we have done so by our own decisions. There's no going back, of course, and I guess most of us wouldn't want to if we could, even though we're acutely conscious of mistakes we've made. We have to remember that each of us is new at this business of living and content ourselves with the fact that most of us have plenty of time to make good decisions in the future.

If there's a rule in making decisions, I suppose it would be to listen to that inner voice and try to make decisions that tend to be growth-oriented. There's really no standing still, even if we'd like to.

I wonder how many mothers in poor families have said to their children, "I want you to get an education and make something of yourselves." The old term "make something of yourself" carries with it the clear message that we invent—that we make—ourselves.

I do think, however, that most try to play it safe, that is, select those decisions that seem to carry the least risk of failure; and by so doing, they live out their lives well below their real potential as persons. Sayings such as "I'm not going to stick my neck out" and "Don't rock the boat"—to say nothing of the popular "Take it easy" and "Never volunteer"—all indicate a reluctance to live fully extended or at the leading edge of life. In business, every time a suggestion is made that involves any sort of innovation, some old-timer will ask, "Who else is doing it?" He needs reassurance that the idea is not completely new, that it's been tested by someone else before he'll venture a "yes" vote.

Professor Sidney Hood writes, "My observations lead me to the conclusion that human beings have suffered greater deprivations from their fear of life than from its abundance."

Developing Two Great Factors

If we would develop heart and mind, learn to love greatly and think clearly, everything else would be added to us— everything we want and more than we need.

THERE'S A SMALL paperback book, edited by Erich Fromm, titled *The Nature of Man*, in which appears the following statement: "People tend to achieve their human potential insofar as they develop love and reason." It might be a good time to ask ourselves how well we're doing in those departments. To the extent that we develop love and reason will we realize our potential as persons. These are the faculties that are uniquely human and on which you and I must depend if we're to achieve what we were designed to achieve.

We tend to think of developing human potential along lines more closely associated with kinds of work or sports, and perhaps that's part of it. But it's the development of heart and mind that can raise us to new levels of humanness. If we would develop heart and mind, learn to love greatly and think clearly, everything else would be added to us—everything we want and more than we need. Most importantly, there would be peace and loving-kindness in all our relations with others.

If you'll think about it, you'll realize that those whose lives are marked by lack in the midst of abundance are those who have not discovered—who have not developed in themselves—the capacities for love and reason.

And if someone should ask you, "How does a person develop his or her potential?" you can reply, "By developing love and reason." With those two capacities alone, the fulfillment is there. We have only to think of the truly great people we have known personally: the great teacher; perhaps a relative, a friend, a parent, a fellow worker, or the stranger who appeared out of nowhere to help us out of a bad situation and who then quietly disappeared, leaving only the memory of a smile and that calm willingness to help.

When we think of the person who has developed love and reason to an uncommonly high degree in his or her life, we invariably think of someone who has a calm, even serene way of looking at things, studying things, before making a decision. Such people give of themselves freely, unstintingly, and they reap an abundant harvest in return. They tend to be quiet people, although they can laugh and enjoy themselves as much as anyone—more, really, because they see more in their surroundings, notice more about the people with whom they associate. They are more understanding and more forgiving and look for the reasons behind events, rather than just at the events themselves.

"People tend to achieve their human potential insofar as they develop love and reason." People with closed minds, on any subject, are stuck somewhere along the way.

Maximizing Your Potential

I'D LIKE TO QUOTE SOMETHING to you from George B. Leonard's excellent book *Education and Ecstasy*. He asks, "Who is this creature we would educate so joyfully? What are his capacities? Can he really be changed? Will great efforts yield great gains? History tells us more than we want to know about what is wrong with man, and we can hardly turn a page in the daily press without learning the specific time, place, and name of evil. But perhaps the most pervasive evil of all rarely appears in the news. This evil, the waste of human potential, is particularly painful to recognize, for it strikes our parents and children, our friend and brothers, ourselves."

James Agee wrote: "I believe that every human being is potentially capable, within his 'limits,' of fully 'realizing' his potentialities; that this, his being cheated and choked of it, is infinitely the ghastliest, commonest, and most inclusive of all the crimes of which the human world can accuse itself. I know only that murder is being done against nearly every individual on the planet."

To doubt is less painful than to rage. Throughout much of history, the safe, the authoritative, the official viewpoint has pronounced man limited, flawed, and essentially unchangeable. Each age has found ways of comforting men with pessimism. Accept limits, the wise men say, to keep from over-reaching yourselves or going mad with hope.

But hope and the awareness of wasted potential have never really faded from consciousness. Ever since the race of man first learned to wonder, men have been haunted by this irrepressible dream: that the limits of human ability lie beyond the boundaries of the imagination; that every human being uses only a tiny fraction of his abilities; that there must be some way for everyone to achieve far more of what is truly his to achieve. History's greatest prophets, mystics, and saints have dreamed even more boldly, saying that all men are somehow one with God. The dream has survived history's failures, ironies, and uneven triumphs, sustained more by intuition than by what our scientific-rationalist society calls "facts."

Now, however, the facts are beginning to come in. Science has at last turned its attention to the central questions of human capability, has begun the search for a technology as well as a science of the human potential. Men in varied fields, sometimes unknown to each other, sometimes disagreeing on method, philosophy, and even language, are coming to startlingly similar conclusions that make pessimism about the human prospect far more difficult than before. These men—neurologists, psychologists, educators, philosophers, and others—are making what may well be the century's biggest news. Almost all of them agree that people now are using less than 10 percent of their potential abilities. Some put the figure at less than 1 percent. The fact of the matter is that anyone who makes a responsible and systematic study of the human animal eventually feels the awe that moved Shakespeare to write, "What a piece of work is a man! How noble in reason! How infinite in faculty!"

The No. 1 Quality for Success

IN TALKING ABOUT IDEAS that we may want to pass along to our kids, in school and more importantly in the home, of all of the qualities that parents can instill in children, which would you say is the most important? Some time back, the editors of a business magazine concluded a survey on what qualities it takes to be successful, but since the survey was by the editors of a business magazine, it was naturally assumed that what was meant is success in business.

Well, interestingly enough, the same No. 1 quality emerged for success in business that came up for success as a father or mother. And do you know what that single quality is? One word: integrity.

There are millions today who will laugh at that, but the odds are good that neither they nor their youngsters are doing too well.

Children who are taught the importance of integrity never seem to lose it. It becomes a part of their being, their way of doing things, and more than anything else, it will guarantee their success in life as persons.

Integrity is what a man wants in his wife and she in him. That's what we look for and hope for in a doctor or dentist, the person who designs and builds our home, the person we work for, and the people who work under us. It's what we want more than anything else in a politician or an appointed official, in judges and police officers.

Integrity is honesty—but much more than the superficial kind of honesty that keeps a person from stealing or cheating. Integrity is a state of mind and character that goes all the way through like good solid construction.

And integrity, or the lack of it, is generally taught in the home, in little as well as in big things. In business or in life, the No. 1 quality is integrity.

For most people, it would seem getting through life is a matter of managing a compromise between integrity and expediency. Integrity is all well and good, and everybody would like to have the word apply to her, but there are times when people think it's perhaps best to wink at integrity and indulge in a little larceny or remain silent—times when speaking one's mind might result in a loss of popularity or ostracism of some kind.

As José Ortega y Gasset tells it, "The human creature is born into the world in a natural state of disorientation. He's the only creature on earth who is not at home in his environment. He must and he does, in a godlike fashion, create his own life, his own world."

Now that's an awesome thing to think about. The responsibility is onerous, frightening. To prevent a white knight-like façade of unblemished and unsoiled integrity is not only difficult; to most people, I'm sure, it's also a little ridiculous. The old battle cry of the mob is, "Everybody does it. Why shouldn't I?" And that's exactly why the person of integrity doesn't do it. The crowd will ask, "What are you trying to be—a boy scout?" What's wrong with being a boy scout? Why shouldn't we go straight in a time when such an attitude needs all the recruits it can get?

Integrity in business is the surest way on earth to succeed. Sometimes it might seem that what you're doing is going to cut into profits, but it inevitably ends up increasing profits.

When we put the well-being of people in first place, we'll never make a mistake. People first, profit last. And the more you do it, the bigger and better your profits become. It's the old law of cause and effect. In my opinion, there should be courses on integrity.

Someone once wrote that if honesty didn't exist, it ought to be invented as the best means of getting rich.

But kids don't learn integrity when they see their father bringing home loot from his place of employment, or bragging about how he cheated on his income tax, or lifting towels and other loose impediments from a hotel or motel room.

In a product, a service, or a human being, integrity is priceless and can only lead to success in the long run. We've all played golf with people who conveniently forget strokes. They fool no one, least of all the other club members, and they become objects of derision. And every week we read in the newspapers of men, quite often in high places, whose lack of basic integrity has landed them in trouble with the law, with resulting damage to themselves and the members of their family. They were not taught the importance of integrity as youngsters and failed to mature and learn the importance of it as adults.

How to Act Like a Pro

MY OLD FRIEND, Herb True, dropped into my office with some exciting thoughts. There are some people you just can't sit down with without getting all fired up—people who are interested in ideas and people.

He said that the pro, in whatever field he happens to work, doesn't follow standards; he sets them! And the first step toward becoming a pro in anything you want very much to do is to learn the rules.

He went on to say that the amateur is the person who doesn't know the rules, and what's even worse, he doesn't know that he doesn't know the rules.

The amateur, when he fails at what he does, says, "Well, that's the way the cookie crumbles." He finds ways of finding exterior reasons for his failures. We tend to look inside of ourselves to explain our successes and outside of ourselves to explain our failures. But the pro accepts responsibility for his actions.

There's the story of the football coach whose team had won four games in a row. When asked by reporters for his secret, the coach went into detail as to his superior methods of coaching, choosing men, and scouting. The following week, his team lost. When asked why, he said, "It rained." And one reporter asked, "Just on your team?"

The real pro would have said, "They fielded a better team than we did today." But the amateur is always scrambling for excuses. He spends his time looking outside of himself for reasons for his failures that could easily be used to bring about success the next time if he decided to turn pro and learn the rules.

The next mark of the real pro is that he has a definite code of conduct. This code is all set up and working. Whenever he comes upon a situation that violates his code, he passes it up. But he doesn't have to sit around and think about it, or try to rationalize it, or find excuses for doing something he knows very well he should not do. He's got a code of conduct, and he sticks by it.

For example, let's say he's in politics or on the police force. His code is that he will not accept bribes of any kind. If someone offers him a bribe, he instantly refuses it because it is a bribe. The amount of the bribe then becomes totally unimportant. Whether it's five dollars or five million dollars makes not the slightest difference.

Another mark of the pro is that he tries always to distinguish between the urgent and the important. Something may be, or may appear to be, very urgent, but is it really important? Is it important in a permanent, meaningful way? Or is its seeming urgency little more than a needless time consumer? Every act we perform during the day is either goal-achieving, tension-relieving, or unnecessary. The pro keeps an intelligent balance. He does this by making sure that the time he's supposed to be working, he's working. He enjoys his work, and he enjoys his leisure.

Yes, the real pro, in whatever he has chosen to do, does not follow the standards set by others. He sets his own. He knows that the precedents he sets will be broken someday, just as he breaks those that have been established before.

SUCCESS STARTS HERE

Do you possess the characteristics of the "pro"? Do you:

accept responsibility for your actions?

have a definite code of conduct?

distinguish between the urgent and the important?

When was the last time you set standards for your behavior?

Eight Words to Live By

EVER SINCE PEOPLE have been able to communicate, they have compiled words to live by. But the world is still troubled. Take these words: honesty—workmanship—ambition—faith—education—charity—courage. Chances are 4.5 billion people won't agree to live their lives by them. But think how much better your life would be if just one person does. You.

With those eight words—eight concepts, really—you'd have about all the good advice you'd ever need to live a productive, rewarding, satisfying life. Let me go over the words once more.

Honesty: It means honesty in everything we do or say—honesty as a way of life. It's saying, "If it isn't honest, I won't have anything to do with it."

Workmanship: Workmanship is not a male or female word, even though it contains the word "man" in the middle of it. It means doing a job as well as we can do it without becoming neurotically obsessed with it. It's the kind of work one expects from a top professional. It's saying, "Everything I do, I will do to the best of my ability."

Ambition: Ambition is a good thing. It means moving toward something we believe to be worthwhile. Ambition keeps us on the most interesting of journeys. And as we'll find when we fulfill our ambition, the journey is better than the accomplishment. Ambition is the desire to do something, and human beings are at their best when they're doing things. Succeed at what you're now doing, and then move on to your next ambition.

As for the idea of faith, the fourth word in the list, we could talk about that all day. Faith makes everything work, and faith in ourselves and what we believe in is the driving power of our ambition.

And next comes *education*—a very big word that means many things. It's certainly not limited to schooling, although that's important, too. The better our education; the broader, the more comprehensive our knowledge; the better, the richer, the more interesting our lives become, and the more we'll understand the true meaning of the words we're discussing here today.

The next one is *charity*, which is a lot more than giving to the United Way, although that's part of it. It's having an attitude of charity; understanding that the more we share, the more we get, and the more we help and lift up others, the more we are helped and lifted up ourselves.

Responsibility means responsibility for ourselves and our lives. If something's wrong in our lives, chances are we're a big part of the problem.

And of course, *courage*. Courage turns the darkness into bright daylight, problems into possibilities.

Chapter Three

MAKING THE MOST OF OPPORTUNITIES

Acres of Diamonds

SOME STORIES ARE SO GOOD they never grow old. One of them is the old story called "Acres of Diamonds." No one knows who told it the first time. It's supposed to be true, and of course it is in that it's happened thousands of times to thousands of people in thousands of different situations.

But the man who made the story famous, in this country at least, was Dr. Russell Herman Conwell, who lived from 1843 to 1925 and who, by telling the story from one end of the world to the other, raised six million dollars, with which he founded Temple University in Philadelphia and thus fulfilled his dream to build a really fine school for poor but deserving young men.

Dr. Conwell told the story "Acres of Diamonds" more than six thousand times and attracted great audiences wherever he appeared. I'm sure you're as familiar with the story as I am. But it isn't the story that's so important in itself; the important thing is that we apply the principle of the story to our own lives.

The story is about a farmer who lived in Africa at the time diamonds were discovered there. When a visitor to his farm told him of the millions being made by men who were discovering diamond mines, he promptly sold his farm and left to search for diamonds himself.

He wandered all over the continent, found no diamonds, and as the story has it, finally penniless, in poor health, and despondent, threw himself into a river and drowned.

Long before this, the man who had bought the farm found a large, unusual-looking stone in the creek-bed that ran through the farm and put it on his mantel as a curio. When the same visitor who had told the original farmer about the diamond discoveries stopped by one day, he examined the stone and told the new owner that he had discovered one of the largest diamonds ever found and that it was worth a king's ransom. To his surprise, the farmer told him the entire farm was covered with stones of that kind. And to make a long story short, if it isn't already too late, the farm that the first farmer had sold so that he could go look for diamonds turned out to be one of the richest diamond mines in the world.

The point Dr. Conwell made was that the first farmer had owned acres of diamonds but had made the mistake of not examining what he had before he ran off to something he hoped would prove to be better.

He would then point out that each of us is like that first farmer. No matter where we live or what we do, we are surrounded by acres of diamonds if we'll simply look for them. Like the curious-appearing stones that covered the farm, they might not appear to be diamonds at first glance, but a little study, a deeper examination, and some polishing will reveal our opportunities for what they really are.

The experts say that each of us has deep reservoirs of ability that we habitually fail to use simply because we fail to develop ourselves to our true stature, and there is lurking in our daily work, as well as in ourselves, acres of diamonds.

We See the World We Look For

AMONG THE WRITINGS of Henry David Thoreau, I came across this statement: "Many an object is not seen, though it falls within the range of our visual ray, because it does not come within the range of our intellectual ray." In other words, there are many things that exist in our world that we don't see because we are not looking for them or perhaps even aren't capable of looking for them. So in the largest sense, the world we see is only the world we look for.

Show two people the same picture, and each will see a different scene; each will extract from what he sees that which he happens to be predisposed to look for. Different people looking out of a train window as they pass through the outskirts of a city will see the same thing from entirely different viewpoints. One will see a depressing, run-down neighborhood. Another will see an ideal plant site. Still another might see a marvelous opportunity for real-estate development. The passing scene might give someone else the idea for a story or a song or a poem. Another, his face buried in a magazine, will see nothing.

The world presents to each of us, every day, that which we seek. There is not a neighborhood or area that does not offer abundant opportunity to every person living there. That opportunity is limited only by the viewpoint of the inhabitant.

Some years ago, a Wisconsin farmer was stricken with polio and left paralyzed in an iron lung. Flat on his back, unable to farm his land, he was forced to push back his intellectual horizon; he was forced to think creatively, to take mental inventory of his assets and liabilities. Without moving from his bed, he built one of the country's largest and most successful meat-packing companies. Unable to use his hands and feet, he was forced to use his most precious, priceless possession—his mind—and he found his farm contained all the riches he and his family would ever need. Where before there was only a farm, now there are great packing plants employing thousands.

I am sure that when his friends and neighbors learned of his affliction, they wondered how he would manage to operate his farm and care for his family. He simply looked at the farm with new eyes; he saw what he had failed to see before, even though nothing had changed except his own mobility.

Every one of us lives in a kind of iron lung of his own fashioning. Each one of us has opportunities just as great as that Wisconsin farmer's. But few of us are forced to reach so far into the deep reservoirs of ability within us. And fewer still know the job of excitement and never-ending interest that can be found in our daily lives when we learn to look at our world as Thoreau looked as his. Surrounded by miracles and limitless opportunity, some people manage to find only boredom and insecurity.

As Thoreau said, we find only the world we look for.

The Value of Maintaining High Expectations

ONE TIME WHEN I WAS IN New York City, my plane was canceled because of mechanical difficulties. More than one hundred of us, I suppose, were left to scramble for another flight to our destinations on a busy, crowded afternoon. I went back to the counter, and a woman told me there was another flight in just an hour.

"Won't that be filled?" I asked.

"Maybe not," she said.

I thought of all the people on my canceled flight fighting for seats on the next one, which was already probably completely booked, and I toyed with the idea of staying overnight and making a new reservation for the following morning.

"Why don't you try it?" she said.

The thought of standing around the airport for another hour only to be turned away from a full flight was very unappealing. "Do you think there's any hope at all?"

"Try it," she said.

So I tried it. I wound up with a window seat up front and was only an hour late arriving at my destination. If I hadn't tried it, I would have had to taxi all the way back into the city, register at a hotel, spend the night, and repeat the whole process the next day. I'd been saved all that by a woman who suggested that I try it. And I resolved to stop giving up so easily—to keep my expectations alive, to expect more.

This is a small example, but we should never lose sight of the undeniable fact that there is a very thin line, if any at all, between what we expect from life and what we get.

If we're not getting what we'd like, maybe it's because our expectations are too low; maybe we're suffering from the poverty of expectation. Your life will come pretty close to matching your expectations. It can easily exceed them. Lower expectations keep us from trying. Higher expectations keep us pressing upon ourselves; they keep us from giving up.

When I was a kid, I remember hearing the words, "If you don't expect much, you won't be disappointed when you don't get much." But that's just the problem: if you don't expect much, you're ruling out the chance of winning. The world is full of people who don't have much because they don't expect much. They're not trying for more, so how in the world are they going to get more?

We should never be concerned about the opportunities we've missed in the past. There's no way on earth to make the most of every opportunity. It's almost never too late, and there will be just as many good opportunities in the future as there have been in the past.

No one is without hope. Every person has expectations of some kind. But just as we tend to underestimate ourselves, we therefore expect too little. We have expectations, but are they high enough? As Goethe put it, "In all things it is better to hope than to despair."

It might be a good idea to take inventory of our expectations. Maybe we could use a new shipment.

We become what we habitually think about!

SUCCESS STARTS HERE

Take time to review your own goals and expectations.

Have you set your sights high enough?

Are you giving up on something that deserves more of an effort?

The Fundamental Principle of Human Action

I READ A COMMENT IN *Forbes* magazine by Henry George. He said, "The fundamental principle of human action is that men seek to gratify their desires with the least exertion."

There's the rub. There's the difference between what we say we want and what we're willing to settle for. It's like the high-school kid who tells his counselor that he wants to be a physician but whose grades are Cs and Ds. Sure, he wants to be a doctor, but only if there isn't too much hard work involved.

I've often thought that therein also lies the crux of the mid-career identity crisis so common among people. You wake up one morning—usually a rainy Monday—look at yourself in the mirror before you've showered and dressed, and get a world-record sinking feeling. You're forty, and you suddenly realize those insurance people know what they're talking about when they deal in mortality tables and that there's one whopping disparity between what you've accomplished and what you used to think you'd accomplish.

"What happened?" you wonder. "Where did all those years go?"

And what have you been doing all that time? And, more importantly, where are you going? What about all those young dreams? Voilà! Identity crisis—you're not the person you intended to become.

And what happened was that you were comfortable; you had a job you could handle with raises along the way, three square meals a day, a family (these are not in the order of their importance, necessarily), a house—well, actually, it was what the others were doing, too. And then those young dreams had been a bit amorphous, a little fuzzy around the edges. The thing is that while you may not be the person you intended to become, you are the person you settled for. You really have what you wanted after all.

I had a call the other day from an older woman I know, and she said, "You know, when I was a girl, I wanted more than anything to learn to play the piano, but my parents couldn't afford it. And there was a super private school I wanted to go to, but they couldn't afford that, either."

I asked her if she had learned to play the piano later on, after she left home. She said, "No." I reminded her that she could have learned to play every instrument in the Boston Symphony during the time she'd wasted since then. I told her that blaming her parents was the easy way out. People who would love to play an instrument or seek a good education can do it one way or another, even if they have to teach themselves, as countless individuals have proven.

So I won the argument and infuriated a nice woman. I had exploded a myth she'd been clinging to for forty years. And I reminded her that there was still plenty of time.

I'd Give Anything to Do What You Do

AN ACCOMPLISHED WOMAN MUSICIAN gave a great piano performance for a women's club. Afterward, over coffee, an admirer from the audience gushed to the virtuoso, "I'd give anything to play as you do."

The woman who had given the concert took a sip of her coffee and fixed the red-faced admirer with a cold glare. And then she said, "Oh, no, you wouldn't!"

A hush fell over the group, coffee cups stopped on their way to and from saucers, and the culprit twitched in sudden embarrassment. Looking about her, she repeated—but in a softer voice—her original statement: "I would too give anything to play the piano as you do." The virtuoso continued to sip her coffee and shake her head. "No, you wouldn't," she repeated. "If you would, you could play as well, possibly better, possibly a little worse, than I do. You'd give anything to play as I do, except time—except the one thing it takes to accomplish the fact. You wouldn't sit and practice hour after hour, day after day, year after year."

Then she flashed a warm smile. "Understand," she said, "I'm not criticizing you. I'm just telling you that when you say you'd give anything to play as I do, you really don't mean it. You really don't mean it at all."

In the pause that followed, a napkin falling to the thick rug would have rattled the windows. The women looked at each other and then back at their coffee cups. They realized that this woman had spoken the truth. It would be nice to have her talent now, fully matured and developed. But as for putting in the twenty years of work that went into the fashioning of it, no; that was a different matter.

Soon, the light conversation was resumed, and the incident was glossed over but not forgotten.

People are forever saying, "I'd give anything…" But the fact remains that they don't. They give very little, often nothing, to do the things they say they'd give anything to do.

The actor who envies the pinnacles reached by the stars, the small business owner, the homemaker, the student, the golfer, the professional persons, the aspiring writer, the painter—across the entire spectrum of achievement, the stars are those who have simply given their dedication, their singleness of purpose, their days and nights, weeks and months and years. And when the harvest they have so painstakingly sown and nurtured for so long begins to be reaped, there are others, with the same time, the same opportunity, the same freedom, who come up to say, "I'd give anything to be able to do what you're doing, to have the things you have."

But as the pianist said, "I'm just telling you that when you say you'd give anything to play as I do, you really don't mean it. You really don't mean it at all."

Each of us has the time and the opportunity. If we say we haven't, we're trying to kid ourselves. Everybody ought to become great at something. What is it that you would give anything to become? Then give it, and you'll become it.

Sometimes it seems as though there are far too many spectators and not enough players. Maybe we're so busy watching the world and everyone else that we forget we have one of our own to win.

What Kind of Ship Are You?

The better prepared, the more skilled and experienced we become, the larger the opportunity we can handle because we've learned to handle the problems that go with it. But at the same time, you can't handle a large opportunity if you permit yourself to be bothered by small problems.

OPPORTUNITIES AND PROBLEMS come in all sizes, from the very small to the very large. There's no such thing as an opportunity without problems or problems without opportunities; they're two sides of the same coin. But it's how we react to them that determines what sort of people we are and how serene or frustrated, successful or unsuccessful, we ultimately become.

Look at it this way: the better prepared, the more skilled and experienced we become, the larger the opportunity we can handle because we've learned to handle the problems that go with it. But at the same time, you can't handle—you might not even recognize—a large opportunity if you permit yourself to be bothered by small problems. If a person is to mature—to reach his full stature as a human being—he must learn to sail over the thousands of small, unimportant problems and irritations that beset all of us. If he permits himself to become involved with the numerous small, unimportant vexations, petty arguments, real or imagined personal slights, the interminable minutiae of life, he'll spend all the years of his life in the shallows.

As we've said before, a person is only as large as the things he lets bother him; he's only as big as the things he lets interest him.

In discussing this not long ago, I got to thinking that people are like sailing craft, and you can compare life itself to an ocean. Now, think of the people you know—and think of yourself—as vessels. The smallest would be a little skiff that bounces and bobs even in calm weather over the smallest waves. It isn't safe to go to sea in a boat that small; it will be swamped by the first large wave that comes along.

From the smallest vessel, let's go now to the largest ocean liner. It doesn't even feel the small waves in the harbor. Not until it reaches the great swells of the open sea does it begin to compensate for roll and pitch. And even the worst storms find it equal to the task. It might arrive in port a day or two late, but it will get there safely, with its passengers and cargo.

What kind of vessel are you? Are you the big liner that sails serenely and confidently far out into the deep, open sea—that pays no attention to the small or even medium-sized waves that break and disintegrate against its tall sides? Or are you the small rowboat that bobs and rocks in the slightest breeze?

As James Allen so beautifully put it, "The strong, calm person is always loved and revered. He is like a shade-giving tree in a thirsty land or a sheltering rock in a storm. Who does not love a tranquil heart; a sweet-tempered, balanced life? It does not matter whether it rains or shines or what changes come to those possessing these blessings, for they are always sweet, serene, and calm. That exquisite poise of character which we call serenity is the last lesson of culture; it is the flowering of life, the fruitage of the soul."

Ships and people come in all sizes. We stop to watch and admire the great ships, while the small craft in the harbor attract only a passing glance. What kind of craft are you?

Chapter Four

Treading the Path to Success

Yes, I Will

WHEN THE American team of mountain climbers conquered Mount Everest, an interesting bit of information filtered out.

It seems that before the team left the United States, each of the skilled mountain climbers was questioned at length by a psychiatrist. And he made it a point to ask each of them this question: "Will you get to the top of Everest?"

As he did, he found each of them answering with enthusiasm with lines such as: "I'm going to do my best," or "I'm going to sure try," or "I'm going to work at it." Of course, each of them knew of Everest's formidable reputation and almost impossible peak. But one of the men, a slightly built man, had a different answer.

When the psychiatrist asked him, "Will you get to the top?" he thought for a moment and then quietly answered, "Yes, I will."

And he was the first one who made it. The people who got near the top and saw him make the final assault on that fabled peak were amazed that he made it because of the poor climbing conditions prevailing at the time.

"Yes, I will." I suppose those three small words, quietly spoken or silently resolved, have been responsible for more human achievement than all the other words in the English language.

At sales conventions, salespeople are sometimes asked to set their own production goals for the year ahead. Sometimes each salesperson is given two cards on which he writes down the amount of business he'll sell during the next twelve months. One card is handed in, and he keeps the other.

In the case of many of the salespeople, the amount they write down is really nothing more than what they would "like" to sell if everything goes alright, if business conditions stay that way, if they get lucky, and if other interests don't come along to get them off the track.

But for a few in each group, the figure they write on their cards represents what they have made up in their minds to really accomplish. It is the irreducible minimum that they will settle for. And by the end of the year, despite economic conditions or anything else, they will have sold that amount or more.

And it often—and I mean quite often—happens that these salespeople are in the smallest, least attractive territories. They're not smarter than their colleagues; they're just people who take the business of being true to themselves seriously. They have determination and endurance, and they wind up winning all the marbles. They also wind up moving ahead in their companies and finally find themselves with the best, highest-paying jobs, while the other salespeople are still writing down production figures they don't take seriously and wondering how old Charlie got to be the vice president in charge of sales.

They should learn three quietly spoken words: "Yes, I will." And they would find themselves getting lucky; they would find themselves selling more, making a lot more money, and having a lot more fun doing it.

Nothing in the world will take the place of persistence. And there isn't a record in the world that will not be broken by it. And it all comes from an individual's coming face to face with himself and saying, "Yes, I will."

What Defines the Successful Person

To succeed as persons requires that we become highly productive people to whom quality is more important than quantity. Truly successful people are maturing people who grow more productive and more interesting as they grow older. They never run out of interesting and challenging things to do.

OVER THE YEARS, I've formed a personal opinion or two about who is successful and who isn't. I thought you might like for me to share these ideas.

An education isn't required for great financial achievement. I know multimillionaires who cannot speak or write a correct sentence. But an education is an absolutely essential ingredient if we are to fully enjoy our success. And taking people as a whole, it is the educated segment that tends to succeed, while the uneducated, who outnumber the educated nineteen-to-one, tend to fail, not just financially, but in the other important categories as well.

Successive goals are as important to true success for a person as an education. Unless we have a goal toward which to work and which stretches us to new dimensions in order to achieve it, we tend to become unproductive and unhappy and quite often find ourselves in various kinds of trouble, including poor health.

To succeed as persons requires that we become highly productive people to whom quality is more important than quantity.

Truly successful people have to continue to develop a sense of humor. They seldom take themselves seriously, but they take their work seriously. They tend to be easy-going, easy-to-talk-to, comfortable people who believe that ostentation and putting on airs are signs of mental immaturity.

Successful people make the world go around. They, not the masses who are quick to assume the credit, are the minority that brings us the great innovations and inventions that have helped us cope and adjust to change. They are the innovators—the curious, the questioning, the excited people of the world—and without them we would still be walking about naked in the forests and scratching for nuts and roots.

I'm sure you can add important qualifications to that little list. There has long been a crack-pot theory that in order to be great, one must be slightly cuckoo—a neurotic or even psychotic person—and history is replete with such examples that are presented as proof. But such people tend to be seriously lopsided. They might achieve significant heights in a particular field but fail in all the other important human categories.

In my opinion, and in the opinion of many modern experts such as the late Dr. Abraham Maslow or Carl Rogers, the really successful people tend to succeed in most categories outside their work as well. They tried to be good family men and women, good at sports, with side-ranging interests and enthusiasm. Maslow called them the self-actualizing people because they have the talent or knack of bringing more of their true capacities to the surface. Far from being neurotics, they are often superbly balanced and happy people. Everyone has his own definition of what constitutes success; these ideas form mine.

Do unto Others

FOR THE LAST ONE HUNDRED YEARS, there have been millions of words written about how to succeed. This applies to every department of our lives, personal and professional. They've told us how to walk, how to smile, how to be enthusiastic. Our magazine, newspaper, radio, and television media tell us how to smell good, glow with health, and stay young-looking.

Fine, that's all great. We all want to sell ourselves to those who are important to us—our family, our friends, our boss, our co-workers, and our customers.

Over the past years, I've made hundreds of speeches to sales and business groups of all kinds, in just about every state in the country. And I've made it a point to talk with every top-flight businessperson or salesperson I've met. I've taken enough notes to fill a good-sized garage, trying to draw a composite picture of the really outstanding, successful person. I've talked to old-timers and young ones, fat ones and skinny ones, extroverts and introverts. (Incidentally, you might be interested to know that a very big percentage of the really successful people I've met are miles from being the hearty, back-slapping, give-me-the-microphone-I-want-to-say-a-few-words kind of people. Instead, they're just very nice, warm, friendly people with homes and kids who decided they wanted more out of life than the average person.)

So as the experts say, I've made a survey, and you'll be a little surprised, maybe, by what I've uncovered. You might say that I took everything I've learned from these people and jammed it into a big wine press, squeezed the whole thing down to its very essence, distilled the essences, and like Dr. Curie, I was left with a radiating substance of incredible power. But, as you maybe already know, this glowing, wonderful thing I found wasn't new. In fact, it was incredibly old. Like the sun, it's been renewing itself all these centuries so that it's just as bright and warm and life-giving today as it ever was. When I realized what I'd discovered, I knew I'd seen it somewhere before, so I pulled down an old book from my office shelf and finally found the passage that puts it into better words than I could. You can look it up yourself. It's in Matthew 7:12, and it reads, "Therefore, all things whatsoever ye would that men should do to you, do ye even so to them; for this is the law and the prophets."

It was the Golden Rule.

The so-called secret of the really successful people is treating the people with whom they come in contact as they themselves would like to be treated if the positions were reversed.

Simple, isn't it! It's so simple, as a matter of fact, that it's completely overlooked by the great majority of people. It's the simple, common, everyday things we take for granted that we miss seeing.

Anyway, that's the secret, if you want to call it a secret, of the world's most successful people. They practice one of the world's oldest and best rules.

YOUR SUCCESS STARTS HERE

What Is Failure?

WHAT IS FAILURE? What does a person have to do, or not do, in order to fail—to be designated as a failure? This is an interesting subject. Think about this for a moment:

Herman Melville died in 1891. He wrote the book *Moby-Dick*, the whaling epic with its tremendous metaphysical concept of evil, at the age of thirty. The book was published in 1851, sold a few copies, and then was promptly forgotten except by the limited connoisseurs of creative writing.

Melville lived forty years beyond the publication of *Moby-Dick*. He considered himself and his book a failure, and from a publisher's point of view, Melville was right. Of his other novels, *Billy Budd* remained unpublished for forty years after his death and, like *Moby-Dick*, has since become a literary classic.

Today, sales of Melville's works run into the millions. But there is no retroactive compensation for the author's troubled soul or shoddy purse.

How then shall we measure values, assay excellence, and compensate for obvious neglect and public apathy? Moby-Dick, "the white whale," is dead, but *Moby-Dick*, the novel, lives in imperishable print, and with it, Melville moves into the company of the literary immortals.

This sort of posthumous fame was by no means restricted to Herman Melville. It has happened to a great many men and women. It was true of Henry Thoreau and Edgar Allan Poe. It was also true of Jesus Christ.

So, what is failure? Failure does not come to a person because he is not recognized by the multitudes during his lifetime. Our success or failure has nothing to do with the opinions of others. It has only to do with our opinion of ourselves and what we're doing. Getting back to Thoreau for a moment, when he had to take most of his unsold books back home from his publishers, it didn't seem to bother him at all. In fact, he made the comment that he had a library consisting of over 700 volumes, most of which he had written himself.

The only person who could be called a failure is that person who tries to succeed at nothing. Success, as far as a person is concerned, does not lie in achievement. It lies in striving—reaching—attempting. Any person who decides upon a course of action that he or she deems worthy of himself or herself as a person, and sets out to accomplish that goal, is a success right then and there.

Therefore, failure consists not in failing to reach our goals, but rather in not setting one. Failure consists of not trying. And certainly Melville and all the others who were not recognized until long after their deaths were successful during their lives because of the fact that they strove all their lives and gave to their work the best that was in them. And for every Melville that we read about, there have been millions of men and women—equally successful—of whom we'll never hear; people who didn't write books or try to save the world but who, in their own quiet way, in their own places, gave to what they had chosen the best that was in them.

> **SUCCESS STARTS HERE**
>
> *Are you working with a specific goal in mind?*
>
> *Have you ever turned back from trying something because you were afraid to fail?*
>
> *Set aside time to make a list of all the things you would try to do if you were guaranteed not to fail. Now try them with a new, positive attitude toward failure.*

If You Believe You Can, You Can

YESTERDAY, I got on the subject of success. I mentioned that only a few people, less than 5 percent, achieve what the world calls great success. This could cover great success in any field—being a wife and mother, growing a better rose, or building a fortune of several millions of dollars. Success is an individual thing, and only the person involved can be responsible for what success is to him.

As long as a person is living within the law, both the spirit and the letter, no one has the right to tell any other human being what success should or should not be.

But people who succeed are people who believe they can succeed. Success, until it has been won, is a mental thing. A man has only his mental picture and his belief until he has achieved his goal.

Belief in oneself is one of humankind's most difficult accomplishments. We tend to believe that others can accomplish the things we would like to accomplish but somehow lack the same faith in ourselves.

Why? Well, it's because we're so familiar to ourselves. We know ourselves (or think we do), and it is human nature to accord more ability to a stranger than to someone we know very well.

As individuals, we're conscious of our shortcomings. We remember, consciously and subconsciously, all our little failings and past failures. We're aware of all the thousands of things we cannot do well, and we underestimate our ability in those areas in which we excel. A man is never a hero in his own home, and the same can be said of how we regard ourselves in our own minds.

We should realize it is no more amazing that we should succeed in the things at which we're good than that others should succeed in their fields.

Succeeding in life is like successfully baking a cake. It's a matter of following a recipe. Any attempts at a shortcut may result in a miserable cake. But any human on earth can be successful if he will decide, once and for all, what it is he wants to accomplish—and really define it, write it out right down to the last comma and period—and then go after it, relentlessly, day after day, week after week, month after month, year after year until it is accomplished. Once a person has the recipe for success, it doesn't bother him too much if he finds himself with an occasional setback or failure, any more than a good cook would worry too much or quit baking cakes just because of an occasional flop. Mature, intelligent people realize that failure is just as much a part of success as success is a part of every failure.

C. W. Wendte wrote, "Success in life is a matter not so much of talent or opportunity as of concentration and perseverance." He's right, but it takes belief in yourself to persevere.

How to Get Rich

Now, if you want to get rich, you have only to produce a product or service that will give people greater use value than the price you charge for it. How rich you get will be determined by the number of people to whom you can sell this product or service.

I HAD LUNCH THE OTHER DAY with a friend of mine who is worth in the neighborhood of 200 million dollars, a fortune which he put together from scratch. If he isn't qualified to speak on the subject of how to get rich, I don't know many people who are. So for those who feel it would be fun to get rich, here's how you go about it.

To begin with, understand that you don't have to drive sharper bargains, treat people unfairly, or hurt any human being in the process of getting rich. And understand that you won't get something for nothing. What you must do, in fact, is give to every person with whom you deal more than you take from him.

How is this possible? Well, naturally you can't give every person more in cash market value than you take from him, but you can and must give him more in *use value* than the cash value of the thing involved.

For example, when you buy a good audiocassette program, you receive more in use value by listening to the program and making it a permanent part of your library—to perhaps hear again and share with the members of your family—than the money you parted with in buying it. This means you're happy about the transaction, and so is the publisher and author of the program. In fact, the cassettes might give you a single idea that could significantly advance your career or greatly increase your net worth. But if it is simply a good, enjoyable program, it has more than repaid you for its purchase price.

It's the same with your car, your clothes, your home, an education; with the computer and other high-tech equipment at your office. You get greater use value from these things than their purchase price. And yet, the people who produced these things are quite content with the profits they received for them. So everybody gets what he wants. This is a pretty basic discussion of what makes the wheels turn, but that's what you frequently need—a return to, a reminder of, the basics.

Now, if you want to get rich—and the word *rich* means something different to everyone—you have only to produce a product or service that will give people greater use value than the price you charge for it. How rich you get will be determined by the number of people to whom you can sell this product or service.

It's here that the hardest part of getting rich comes in: you have to think. You have to find a quiet place where you can go every day and be undisturbed. There, with a pad of paper and a pen, jot down your idea. Look for things in which you find an intense interest—things you most love to buy and have yourself. Perhaps there's something for you here, something you can do better than it's now being done. People vote with their money, and they'd vote for you in a minute if you'll give them a greater use value for their money than they're now getting.

Thinking is the one thing everyone has to do on his own. Each of us has a gold mine between his ears; that goes without saying. But digging in it is the world's hardest work. Yet it would richly repay those who go to the trouble to dig in it every day.

People Make the Difference

SOME TIME BACK I had occasion to do some work with the management of one of the country's largest corporations. A few years prior to my having been called in, the company had been in very serious difficulties and had been losing many millions of dollars. Its stock had sunk to a record low price, and many experts felt it to be something of a dinosaur flailing about in its death throes.

Gloom had pervaded the entire organization. The employees, many thousands in number, went about their jobs as though attending a wake, and the company's competitors welcomed its disillusioned customers by the thousands with open arms and racked up new sales records.

Finally, in some desperation, the board of directors fired the company president and hired a new man from another company and gave him broad, sweeping powers of reorganization. He brought in a new management team, and they rolled up their sleeves and went to work.

In almost no time, a new feeling, a new spirit, began to pervade the organization. Slowly, the steady downward turn was brought to a halt, and the company began to show signs of life. Within three years, the company was comfortably back into a very profitable position. It had a new look, a new spirit, and was back into the first rank of world organizations.

The only change had been the management.

The quality, the excellence, the greatness of people had been there all the time, waiting only to be directed, motivated, inspired. This is the job of management, of leadership. It can be an army, a giant corporation, a small business, a classroom, or a family. The people will reflect their leadership, and the success of the group, as a unit, will depend on it.

This is why people in top management in business are so well-paid. It isn't that they're ten times smarter than the people who work under them, or work ten times as hard, or put in ten times as many hours. They are paid, often, ten times as much, because they possess that rare gift of being able to successfully direct the efforts of others and to infuse in the minds and spirits of others the belief that the game can be won instead of lost.

I feel certain that when most people see a great company sprawling across the landscape or see its products at work on every side, they think of it as a giant "thing," an impersonal, mechanical monster that uses human beings much as it uses other raw materials in the shaping of its products.

But that's not the way it is. In reality, it is people that make it work or stand idle; that make it succeed or fail. It is nothing more than a great slave supplying the needs of its customers and under the direction, at every moment, of human minds and hands. And somewhere, in an office with the word "president" on the door, there is a man who is alone responsible for the direction of its destiny.

On the street or at home he might look much like any other man, but that's where the similarity ends. He's the person who directs the people who make the whole thing go. People make the difference.

If You Want It, Just Do It

A FAVORITE EXPRESSION OF James F. Lincoln, the man who built the Lincoln Electric Company, is "You never know what a man can do until he has been given sufficient incentive to strive to his utmost to bring out the God-given abilities within him." How many incipient Fords and Edisons go to their graves unrecognized, the world will never know. The tragedy is, they were never given sufficient incentive—or never met a crisis in their lives that brought out their hidden powers.

And one of the country's outstanding business executives, A. W. Robertson, wrote, "If a man does only what is required of him, he is a slave. The moment he does more than is required, he becomes a free man. We all have work to do in this world; it is the doing of just a little more that leads to happiness and contentment."

It is believed that millions know what they would like to do but are afraid to begin. They feel inadequate. They're afraid they might fail. They believe they lack the necessary ability.

A man named Clifford Echols had dreamed for years of going into business for himself. All his life he'd worked as a clerk in a grocery store, and the highest salary he'd ever made was forty-five dollars a week. One day he ran across a quotation by Emerson that got him off dead center. The quotation was this one: "Do the thing and you will have the power; but they that do not the thing have not the power."

He mortgaged everything he had, arranged for some credit from the necessary suppliers, and a few years later was doing one million dollars a year in business.

He said later, "As I started to do the thing—the thing I'd been thinking and planning to do—I began to discover that I had hidden talents I had never suspected. Ideas came to me that I was able to turn into more successful business. In short, when I had enough faith to start to do the thing, I did find that I had the power. I had had it all along and hadn't realized it."

There's an important lesson here. It is only when we actually begin that we find we have the power and the talent to carry it off. As long as we sit and think about it, wish for it, and stay where we are, nothing happens.

Even Michelangelo said, "If people only knew how hard I worked to gain mastery, it wouldn't seem wonderful at all."

W. Somerset Maugham once wrote, "It's a funny thing about life—if you refuse to accept anything but the best, you very often get it."

And that's about it. We get what we expect from life. If we expect more and plunge in after it, we'll get it. If you want to turn your dreams into reality, you're going to have to take a chance. There's no playing it safe. As long as you keep one foot on first base, it's impossible to get to second. You simply begin, and you will find the ability.

Professor Ashley Montagu put it this way: "Be choosy, therefore, about what you set your heart on; for if you want to achieve it strongly enough, you will."

Chapter Five

WHAT YOU NEED TO KNOW TO SUCCEED

What Happens When You Don't Do Your Best

We need only to perform successfully each act of a single day to enjoy a successful day. If you will do each day only the things you know you should do and do them as well as you can, you can rest assured that you will be successful all the years of your life.

A FORMER NUCLEAR-SUBMARINE OFFICER tells about an interview he had with the distinguished and formidable Admiral Hyman Rickover, the head of the US Submarine Service. Here's the story in his words:

"I had applied for the nuclear-submarine program, and Admiral Rickover was interviewing me for the job. It was the first time I had met Admiral Rickover, and we sat in a large room by ourselves for more than two hours. He let me choose any subject I wished to discuss. Very carefully, I chose those about which I knew the most at the time—current events, seamanship, music, literature, naval tactics, electronics, gunnery—and he began to ask me a series of questions of increasing difficulty. In each instance, he soon proved that I knew relatively little about the subject I had chosen.

"He always looked right into my eyes, and he never smiled. I was saturated with cold sweat. Finally, he asked me a question, and I thought I could redeem myself. He said, 'How did you stand in your class at the Naval Academy?' Since I had completed my sophomore year at Georgia Tech before entering Annapolis as a plebe, I had done very well, and I swelled my chest with pride and answered, 'Sir, I stood fifty-ninth in a class of 820!' I sat back to wait for the congratulations—which never came. Instead, Admiral Rickover asked another question: 'Did you do your best?'

"I started to say, 'Yes, sir,' but I remembered who this was and recalled several of the many times at the Academy when I could have learned more about our allies, our enemies, weapons, strategy, and so forth. I was just human. I finally gulped and said, 'No, sir, I didn't always do my best.'

"He looked at me for a long time and then turned his chair around to end the interview. He asked one final question, which I have never been able to forget—or answer. He asked, 'Why not?' I sat there for a while, shaken, and then slowly left the room."

The former submarine officer who told that story was Jimmy Carter, former governor of Georgia and president of the United States.

Admiral Rickover made a lot of people nervous in his presence and as a result of his questions. But with regard to the question, "Did you do your best?" how would you stack up these days? In the midst of world competition managed by bright, hardworking people, we must do our best—every day, all over again.

Our job, then, is to play out the role we have undertaken to the best of our ability. Success is nothing more or less than this. We become dull or bored or uneasy with ourselves only when we shirk what we know full well we should be doing. The happiest and most contented people are those who, each day, perform to the best of their ability.

A lifetime consists of years, months, weeks, and days. The basic unit of a lifetime is a single day. And a single day in our careers is made up of certain acts that each of us must perform. We need only to perform successfully each act of a single day to enjoy a successful day. If you will only do each day the things you know you should do and do them as well as you can, you can rest assured that you will be successful in all the years of your life.

You don't have to run around in circles trying to do a great many things. It is not the number of acts you perform but rather the efficacy with which you perform the ones you do that counts. Don't try to do tomorrow's or next week's work today. Just do today's as best you can, and leave tomorrow's for tomorrow. And remember that it's important not to slight a single act during the day, because sometimes we do not know how really important some little act may be.

The Turning Point

O N A RECENT PROGRAM I mentioned that there must be thousands of people every day who, without realizing they're on the brink of success, give up in failure. It reminded me of something Dr. A. J. Cronin once wrote, so I dug it out. Here's part of it. Because of his health, Dr. Cronin had to give up his career in medicine, so he turned to writing. He took a room on a small farm in Scotland and for months toiled away on the manuscript of a book. Here's what he wrote:

"When I was halfway through, the inevitable happened. A sudden desolation struck me like an avalanche. I asked myself, 'Why am I wearing myself out with this toil for which I am so preposterously ill-equipped? What's the use of it?' I threw down my pen. Feverishly I read over the first chapters which had just arrived in typescript from my secretary in London. I was appalled. Never, never had I seen such nonsense in all my life. No one would read it. I saw, finally, that I was a presumptuous lunatic, that all that I had written, all that I could ever write was wasted effort, sheer futility. Abruptly, furiously, I bundled up the manuscript, went out and threw it in the trash can.

"Drawing a sullen satisfaction from my surrender, or, as I preferred to phrase it, my return to sanity, I went for a walk in the drizzling rain. Halfway down the loch shore, I came upon old Angus the farmer, patiently and laboriously ditching a patch of the bogged and peaty heath which made up the bulk of his hard-won little farm. I told him what I had done and why. His weathered face scanned me with disappointment and a queer contempt, and he said, 'No doubt you're right, doctor, and I'm the one that's wrong...' He seemed to look right to the bottom of me. 'My father ditched this bog all his days and never made a pasture. I've dug it all my days and I've never made a pasture. But pasture or no pasture,' and he put his foot on the spade, 'I cannot help but dig. For my father knew and I know that if you only dig enough, a pasture can be made here.'

"I understood. Drenched, shamed, furious, I trampled back to the farm, picked the soggy bundle from the trash can, and dried it in the kitchen oven. Then I flung it on the table and set to work again with a kind of frantic desperation."

Well, to make a long story short, that manuscript that A. J. Cronin threw into the trash can and then reclaimed and rewrote was *Hatter's Castle*. It earned him a fortune and made him famous, but far more importantly, it brought him the greatest triumph anyone can achieve—victory over himself. He went on to produce *The Citadel*, *The Keys of the Kingdom*, and so many other popular books—many of which were also made into motion pictures. But nothing gave him the intense satisfaction of that first great success—his conquest over doubt and despair.

What might have happened if he had not come across the farmer that night? The world might have been denied a great author, and he would have missed the greatest success and satisfaction possible. It makes you wonder just how many stop too soon...quit too early in the game.

Each of us has a perfectly natural tendency to underestimate our own power, to feel despair, to want more than anything else to quit. That's the time we should not quit.

YOUR SUCCESS STARTS HERE

The Right to Fail

Only those individuals who are willing to try again after their failures—those who seem to have some strange inner knowledge that success can be theirs if they just stay with it long enough—finally win their diploma in life.

HAS LIFE EVER SHOWN YOU that the right to fail is as important as the right to succeed? If we didn't have bad weather, we would never appreciate sunny days. One hardly ever values his good health until he becomes ill. And I have never known a successful man or woman whose success did not hinge on some failure or another.

There is an old saying that goes, "It is impossible to succeed without suffering. If you are successful and have not suffered, someone has suffered for you; and if you are suffering without succeeding, it is so that you may succeed later or that someone may succeed after you. But there is no success without suffering."

Success in the world—any kind of success—is like a college degree. It can be earned only by following a certain course of action for a definite period of time. It is impossible for substantial success to be easy.

Success also follows a kind of natural selection. Only those individuals who are willing to try again after their failures, those who refuse to let defeat keep them down for long, those who seem to have some strange inner knowledge that success can be theirs if they just stay with it long enough, finally win their diploma in life.

Most men and women who have earned success will tell you that often, just as they felt they were finally reaching the point in life on which they had set their hearts, the rug was pulled out from under them and they found themselves back at the starting line again—and not just once or twice, but many times.

Thus, only those of patient persistence are rewarded. But those who do not achieve outstanding success in life are by no means failures. They are successful in their way because they have what they really want. They simply did not want great success enough. They're happy with what they've got, and there's nothing wrong with that.

One day a young man came to my office and told me he wanted very much to make a great success of himself. He asked if I could show him the secret.

I told him to decide definitely upon what he considered success to be for him, and then work at it for twelve to sixteen hours a day until he had achieved it—and when he wasn't working at it, to think about it. By doing this, he could reach his goal. However, to achieve success, he must force himself back on the track every time he strayed off, realizing that failures are as necessary to success as an excavation is to a basement.

I never saw that young man again. I wonder if he took my advice. It is an unusual person whose desire is larger than his distaste for the work involved.

Successful people are dreamers who have found a dream too exciting, too important, to remain in the realm of fantasy. Day by day, hour by hour, they toil in the service of their dream until they can see it with their eyes and touch it with their hands.

Growth or Decay

HAVE YOU EVER WONDERED why a man keeps growing even after he's what the world considers to be successful? Or a successful business—why does it keep growing long after it's reached great success?

I know of a business firm that each year does several billions of dollars' worth of business. If I mentioned its name, it would be as familiar to you as your own. At a recent meeting, I gave a talk to the company's management, people brought in from all over the country and from some countries abroad. Afterwards, the executive in charge of the meeting was outlining the company's plans for the coming year, and a part of these plans included some really substantial growth. The company was shooting for sales goals that would have appeared ridiculous a few years before. And they were realistic goals, and they will be reached.

But, you might wonder, why? What does a company doing billions of dollars' worth of business—millions of dollars a month—keep setting higher goals for itself, continue to expand, and build and hire more people and get bigger?

Intelligent business people realize that a business is either growing or decaying. There's no such thing as standing still. You can never reach a place where you say, "This is it. We're as successful as we want to be; now we'll just hold the fort and maintain our present volume and profit." There are too many variables. As Sir Isaac Newton proved in his laws of physics, a body in motion tends to remain in motion. And a stationary body tends to remain stationary. If a business or a person stood still and the rest of the country and the economy and the world continued to advance, it would constitute a situation in which the business or the person would, whether he liked it or not, be going backwards. If everything in the world stood still at the same time, it might be alright, but this is never the case. Our competition is not standing still. The times are changing. Tastes and likes and dislikes of the customer change. And we must change and grow with them or die.

If a successful man should consider himself to be as successful as he wants to be, and if he would collect his marbles and quit, what then? What happens to his habits of hard work—of creative thinking and activity that he's devoted many years to develop? What happens to his enthusiasm for an exciting project?

Unless he soon throws himself into something challenging and interesting, he will begin to retrogress, to shrink, to die. He can't stand still even if he wants to. Nor can anything in nature. A tree—any tree at any time—is either growing or decaying, and a business or a human works the same way.

This is why the successful small business tends to grow into a successful large business, and successful large businesses tend to grow larger. It's good for everyone concerned. It creates more jobs, more wealth, more productivity, more growth, and a higher standard of living for everyone.

If you find yourself standing still, watch out.

When Opportunity Knocks, Are You Ready?

Succeeding in life is not a matter of luck or chance or circumstance but only a matter of preparation—of doing what you are given to do each day the best you can and holding firm to the certain knowledge that your time will come and you'll be ready for it when it does.

A YOUNG AND ASPIRING ACTOR once asked Eddie Cantor for advice on getting ahead in show business. The veteran comedian thought for a moment and then answered him in one word: "Prepare."

Opportunity comes to most people many times, in many ways. The question is not so much when and how it will come but whether we'll be ready for it when it does come—whether or not we'll even recognize it.

People today who complain about a lack of opportunity are generally the kind of people who have the mistaken idea that the world owes them a living. They're generally the people who sit around waiting for something wonderful to happen to them, with no particular effort on their part. In fact, many people still hold the mistaken idea that it's not what you know but who you know. They couldn't be more wrong, and as long as they cling to this worn-out, old alibi, they're their own worst enemy.

If you'll examine the lives of men and women whom people call lucky, you'll find that their luck consisted of painstaking preparation and indefatigable persistence. They are, almost without exception, men and women who had something they wanted very much to do and who somehow knew they could do it if they'd only stay with it long enough.

That's what Eddie Cantor meant when he gave his success formula for show business in one word: "Prepare." Because if a person will prepare, he can do so in the calm certainty that his opportunity will come and that he'll be ready for it when it arrives.

It's all a matter of doing certain things a certain way every day. That's all there is to it. I think our young people in school should be taught this fact: that succeeding in life is not a matter of luck or chance or circumstance, but only a matter of preparation—of doing what you are given to do each day the best you can and holding firm to the certain knowledge that your time will come and you'll be ready for it when it does.

Giving a person an opportunity when he has not prepared for it makes him look ridiculous. And the people who complain about the lack of opportunity are only indicating to the world that they are not prepared, not qualified, for opportunity, because it is all around them every day of their lives.

The Turks have a proverb that goes, "The devil temps all other men, but idle men tempt the devil." I wonder how much dissatisfaction in the world could be traced to not having enough to do or not doing enough of what we should be doing.

The Drowning of Mr. and Mrs. Elbert Hubbard

Dear Sirs:

From the latest intelligence that I can get from the Cunard office, I fear that Mr. and Mrs. Elbert Hubbard on the Lusitania are not amongst us who were more fortunate, and as a fellow passenger on that boat, and as one who has known Mr. Hubbard for years, may I express to you my deepest sympathy in your sudden and terrible bereavement.

It may be some satisfaction to you to know that Mr. Hubbard and his wife met their end calmly and serenely, together. I am confident of this, for I was standing talking to them by the port rail directly near the bridge, when the torpedo hit the ship on the starboard side. I turned to them and suggested their going to their stateroom on the deck below to get life belts, but Mr. Hubbard stood by the rail with a half smile on his face and with one arm affectionately around his wife. She was quietly standing beside him, and no sense of fear was shown by either of them.

I went to my stateroom and got several life belts and came back to the place where I had left them, but I did not see them, nor did we meet again on the boat.

These are poor words of consolation at a time like this, but I trust they will be acceptable to you. I never saw two people face death more calmly or almost happily, for they were speaking together quietly, and each seemed to have a happy smile on his and her face as they looked into each other's eyes.

Yours very sincerely,

C. E. Lauriat, Jr.

And that was the way it ended for Elbert Hubbard, writer, editor, and printer, who, at the time, was one of the world's most famous men, and his wife, Alice. They were never seen again. One of the last things Elbert Hubbard had written was his definition of a successful person.

Elbert Hubbard's definition of a successful person was as follows: "He has achieved success who has worked well, laughed often, and loved much."

Chapter Six

Finding Happiness in Life

Understanding Discontent

A PERSON CAN GO A LONG WAY toward alleviating and understanding his discontent if he will understand the perverse nature of the human being. When a person works too hard, or just works steadily for a long time, he becomes discontented and wants rest and relaxation. When he relaxes too long, he seeks work. When he is around too many people for too long, he longs for solitude. When he's alone too long, he longs for human companionship. The young envy the older person and long for the years to quickly pass. The older envy the young and often wish they could somehow turn back the clock of time.

You'll be a lot happier and have a much better sense of humor if you'll understand that it is an integral and indissoluble part of human nature to become dissatisfied, to want what you don't have at the moment. Moments of complete and blissful satisfaction are wonderful but rare and soon give way to a nagging desire for something else. And that's good.

If we understand this part of ourselves, we can avoid frustration. It is this godlike discontent that lurks in the growing person that is responsible for all human progress. That our discontent is also responsible for a great deal of pain and unnecessary suffering is simply the other side of the coin.

Do you remember the old fable about the fisherman who caught a magic prince in the form of a fish? The fish told the fisherman that if he'd let him go, the fish would grant any wish. The fisherman let him go, talked it over with his wife, and they started wishing. Each time their wish was granted, they'd then wish for something greater. Finally, they lived in a great gleaming castle, with hundreds of servants, but it wasn't enough. The wife wanted then to control the sun, to make it obedient to her whim. When the fisherman asked for this wish, the finny prince was disgusted and took away everything. They were once again in the simple shack.

Like so many old fables, it's a commentary on human nature, and it comes uncomfortably close to the truth. We say, "If only I had such and such, I'd be completely happy for the rest of my life." It isn't true. As soon as we have such and such for a while—a surprisingly short while—we then want something else. Discontent comes with the territory; it comes with being human.

As you discontented? If you are, that's good. That's why we're not still squatting in a filthy, drafty cave and grunting and scratching. Divine discontent—to understand it is to use it properly.

The Smell of Horses

I WAS STAYING AT A RESORT HOTEL—the Grand Hotel on Mackinac Island in northern Michigan. One evening after dinner, I settled myself comfortably in a chair on the porch that runs the entire length of the old frame hotel—supposedly, it's the longest porch in the world—just to relax and enjoy the delightful evening. There was a light breeze and a good moon. The lake was beautiful, and the lights of the passing ships could be seen. The evergreens stood out clearly in the moonlight, and it was altogether one of those really great nights you remember.

Before long, a young couple came strolling down the long porch. They were walking arm in arm, and I thought that they were all that was needed to make the picture complete. They walked slowly by me and then took seats not far away. They were silent for a moment, and I naturally thought that they were enjoying the remarkable beauty of the scene and the night as much as I was, when the young woman spoke. I know these were her exact words, because I wrote them down as soon as I could stop laughing. She said, "I hate the smell of horses."

There are no automobiles on Mackinac Island. Horses are the only method of transportation, and they naturally lend their own unique flavoring to the island's atmosphere. I found it charming and a lot less irritating than the noise and fumes of cars, taxis, and trucks.

But what made me laugh, of course, was that in the midst of all that beauty, on one of the most beautiful evenings of the year, in so romantic and charming a setting, the only thing the young woman noticed that was worth mentioning was the faint odor of horses.

They looked at me in surprise when I laughed, so I had to explain why—which neither of them found to be amusing at all. In fact, the young woman seemed somehow offended, and they soon moved away from the strange character who not only eavesdropped but also laughed at them.

The sad thing about it all was that the attractive young woman belongs to that vast army whose members make it their business to spend their lives focusing on the wrong things. I'll bet if the young man gave her a string of pearls, she'd busy herself with a minute inspection of the clasp. On a beautiful day, such people can spot that tiny cloud on the horizon. They don't appreciate the good qualities in people but complain about their defects. If their children bring home report cards with five Bs and one C, it's the C that will get the comments and the attention.

They do not look for what's right but what's wrong. In a world of miracles and beauty, they see only horse droppings. If you mention this to them, they will usually say you have your head in the sand and you have it all backward.

There is nothing in the world that is perfect, and it's our job to eliminate as many defects as we can. But pity the poor people who go through life seeing only the flyspecks on the window of the world.

How to Be Happy

WOULD YOU LIKE TO KNOW how to be happy? The answer, believe it or not, is known, and it took one of the most brilliant minds ever to appear on the earth to come up with the answer. His name was John Stuart Mill, who lived from 1806 to 1873 and became an outstanding philosopher and economist. He is believed to have had perhaps the highest IQ of any person who has ever lived. So, unless you think you're smarter, pay attention.

John Stuart Mill said, "Those only are happy who have their minds fixed on some object other than their own happiness; on the happiness of others, on the improvement of mankind, even on some art or pursuit, followed not as a means, but as itself an ideal end. Aiming thus at something else, they find happiness by the way."

To my mind there is no doubt whatever that that is the true and only path to lasting and meaningful happiness. The definition is so excellent, and people so often seem to be so confused as to what happiness is all about, so let me repeat it: "Those only are happy who have their minds fixed on some object other than their own happiness; on the happiness of others, on the improvement of mankind, even on some art or pursuit, followed not as a means, but as itself an ideal end. Aiming thus at something else, they find happiness by the way."

I wonder why that isn't taught in school. I believe it's safe to say that not one person in 5,000 could give you as intelligent a definition of what true happiness is all about. We must have our minds fixed on something other than happiness in order to find it. If we seek it directly, it will elude us forever.

People say, "I want to be happy" as though it's something that can come to them whether they do anything about it or not. Such people can never know happiness until they break out of the tiny world of themselves. "Those only are happy who have their minds fixed on some object other than their own happiness." Therein lies the secret.

The happiest people are usually the busiest people and almost always those whose business consists of serving others in some way. By losing themselves in what they're doing and where they're going, happiness quietly joins them and becomes part of them.

The miserable, unhappy people who cause such misery and unhappiness to others are the self-centered people, the people who worry constantly about what they're getting rather than what they're giving; and the world is full of them, unfortunately. We see their harried, unhappy, furtive, ferret-like faces everywhere, pushing their grasping hands, extended. They fear life; they fear death. They are the pitiful caricatures of humanity. And they pay a terrible price for their ignorance.

A Mistake in Waiting for Happiness

The fact is that most of the ingredients necessary for happiness are present in the lives of most people every day. They are things and conditions for which we need not wait. And most of them are things we're so used to that we take them for granted.

HAVE YOU EVER NOTICED how most people seem to be waiting to be happy in the future? They seem to be so intent on getting through the day that they forget to enjoy it. It's as though happiness is a distant city to them—a city they're striving to reach. But happiness is something that must be learned and practiced if we're to become skilled at it. Pushing it out into the indeterminate future involves running the risk that we won't know how to be happy when we get there.

It's like saying, "Someday, when I can afford to buy a piano, I'll sit down and play beautiful music." It doesn't work that way. Owning a piano doesn't confer the knowledge of how to play. And arriving at a particular stage of like, whether it's measured in terms of age or income, doesn't mean that we'll suddenly become happy people.

A reporter interviewing J. Paul Getty, who could, at that time, have cashed in his chips for several billion dollars, asked, "Mr. Getty, what is it that money cannot buy?" And he replied, "I don't think it can buy health, and I don't think it can buy a good time. Some of the best times I have ever had didn't cost me any money."

The fact is that most of the ingredients necessary for happiness are present in the lives of most people every day. They are things and conditions for which we need not wait. They are ours today. And most of them are things we're so used to that we take them for granted. They're the people with whom we live and work, our children, our hopes. There's the anticipation of the day and what it will bring—the opportunity to work well and honestly so that we can take pride and satisfaction from it and by so doing enjoy our leisure and our rest. There's the happiness that should come from being with our friends and neighbors. And the thoughtful person finds happiness in just being alive. He enjoys walking on a sunny day, but he likes to walk in the rain, too. He can find happiness from the sound of the surf or the crackling of a fire.

How to Be Miserable

LET ME GIVE YOU SOME TIPS on how to be miserable. Don't laugh—there are literally millions of people who wouldn't trade their daily misery for all the gold in the world. You may know some of them. In fact, if you know ten people, you probably know several of these misery lovers. (This may be an exaggeration, and it may not be, either.)

The first step to real, professional-type, solid, unremitting misery is to get all wrapped up in yourself and your problems—real or imagined. Become a kind of island, surrounded on every side by yourself. By turning all of your thoughts inward upon yourself, naturally you cannot spend much or any time thinking about others and other things. And so, finally, the outside world—the real world—will disappear into a kind of Hitchcock-type fog. You'll know the world is there because every once in a while you'll bump into it; but for the most part, it will be murky and indistinguishable.

And it's right here that you have to understand an important but little-known fact: the type of person who turns inward upon himself doesn't have much in the wisdom department, or he'd never do it; and as a result, he doesn't have much to turn inward upon. He finds a kind of vacuum, and he must then invent things.

He invents things like "the world is against him," which is the worst possible kind of conceit. The world isn't against him; it doesn't even know he exists—and as a result, it ignores him completely.

So, since this person doesn't get too much attention from this attitude, he tries to get attention through various other means. One is to hunt for illness of some kind. If he looks long enough—and it doesn't take long—he can find symptoms of any condition or disease known to man—and some that are unknown—ranging from yaws to rabies. With his newfound illness, he has something with which he hopes to make everyone else as miserable as he is. So he tells them all about it. They don't particularly want to listen, but he tells them anyway and watches for signs of sympathy. And at first he gets it, so he thinks he's got it made, and he keeps it up, with new and interesting medical problems. He wakes up every morning feeling rotten, and he lets the world know about it!

But soon he detects a change. People begin to walk away as he approaches—they don't want to hear his deadly recitation anymore. Even his family turns an uninterested, deaf ear to his protestations of being on the brink of a slow and painful death.

This makes him angry, so, childlike, he cries out that nobody cares whether he lives or dies, and by this time he's pretty close to the truth. So the bitterness deepens, the misery thickens, and he draws farther and farther back into his cave, shouting imprecations at the world, throwing an occasional stone at a passerby, and, in general, making a complete ass of himself.

Well, there you have it—one of the best and most common formulas for being miserable and making those around you miserable, as well. And it all starts with becoming too wrapped up in yourself, feeling that you're important, somehow.

Samuel Johnson wrote, "Many of our miseries are merely comparative; we are often made unhappy, not by the presence of any real evil, but by the absence of some fictitious good." And a Hindu proverb says, "The miserable are very talkative." And they are, aren't they?

The Master Word

I RAN ACROSS SOMETHING INTERESTING called "The Master Word." It's about a word that will work wonders for a person regardless of his age or what he does with his days. Man, woman, or child, the master word will bring meaning and usefulness into his or her life, new clarity and self-respect and satisfaction into the passing days.

This was written by the great physician Sir William Osler:

"Though little, the master word looms large in meaning. It is the 'open sesame' to every portal, the great equalizer, the philosopher's stone which transmutes all base metal of humanity into gold. The stupid it will make bright; the bright, brilliant; and the brilliant, steady. To youth it brings hope; to the middle-aged, confidence; the aged, repose."

Do you know what the master word is? Guess. I used it in the second sentence. Did you recognize it?

Well, the master word is—*work*!

I've talked about this before, but it's been said that we need reminding as much as we need educating. Human beings have the strangest and most perverse tendency to take the best parts of life for granted. In fact, the human being has the capacity to take anything, no matter how great it might be, for granted once he becomes used to it. The actor in front of the cameras, the captain of a great ocean liner, the man at the controls of a giant earth-moving machine, the writer, the painter, the mother all seem to let the charm and excitement of their work fade after a while until it becomes as humdrum to them as candling eggs.

The Byproducts of Life

DR. PAUL SCHERER, speaking of Job's impatience to get immediate and direct answers to his questions, said, "Greatness and peace and happiness are simply not proper ends for any human soul to set for itself. They are the byproducts of a life that has held steady like a ship at sea to some true course worth sailing."

In other words, if the course to which you're holding is right, everything else you want will come as byproducts. How does a person find "some true course worth sailing"?

I remember some time back a man came to me for advice on how he might become a popular, sought-after platform speaker. He told me he enjoyed making speeches and wanted to make a career of it. I asked him what he wanted to say, and he drew a complete blank. It became clear that he was ready to speak on any subject the entertainment committee wanted him to speak on. It wasn't the subject that interested him; it was just that he wanted to make speeches. I told him that he would never become a great and sought-after speaker until he had something he wanted very much to say—something inside him that burned to get out, that he felt needed telling. Speakers become great because of what they want to say; greatness follows the zeal of their subject.

And it's the same with some true course worth sailing. A person needs to find the course in which he can lose himself, dedicate himself. Then the greatness and the peace and the happiness will come to him naturally as the bee comes to the blooming flower or a child runs to its parents.

People who find their lives filled with confusion and uncertainty, with boredom and unhappiness, need to find a meaningful vehicle for their lives—something in which they can lose themselves completely. It need not be some great cause, although it can be. It can be found in our present work, as a rule; it needs only to be ferreted out.

We need to become, in the words of Dr. Abraham Maslow, "self-actualizing." We need to become people who are steadily moving toward fulfillment, toward personal enrichment.

Dr. J. Wallace Hamilton puts it pretty well when he asks and answers his own question. He writes, "What then are the basic laws of happiness, and how do we learn them? I suppose the clearest law upon which there is fundamental agreement is that this inner music of the soul which we have named 'happiness' is essentially and inevitably a byproduct, that it comes invariably by indirection. To pursue it, to pounce upon it, to go directly after it is the surest way not to obtain it."

People who make a mission of seeking happiness miss it, and people who talk loudly about the right to be happy seldom are. It's a byproduct, an agreeable thing added in the pursuit of something else.

SUCCESS STARTS HERE

Are you doing something with your life that offers you a sense of fulfillment?

What do you love to do most that allows you to forget yourself?

Use this self-knowledge to cheer yourself up the next time you're feeling low.

YOUR SUCCESS STARTS HERE

Plant Your Roots in a Great Moving Current

A person should have his roots deep in a great moving current—a moving stream of conscious direction—which will keep him sailing steadily toward the destination he has chosen regardless of the economic and social winds that blow first this way and then that on the surface.

WAY BACK IN THE DAYS of sailing ships, sailors who entered into Antarctic waters would occasionally see a strange and awe-inspiring sight. They would see a great iceberg towering high out of the sea, moving against the wind. Since they depended on the wind to drive their ships, they were keenly aware of its direction, and to see this great, shining, apparently inanimate monolith of ice moving mysteriously into the teeth of the wind was, to them, uncomfortably curious.

It was not until much later that students of the sea learned of the great currents that, like titanic rivers, moved their mysterious ways through the body of the sea.

These icebergs—some so huge that it took days to sail past them—had their roots, 90 percent of their bulk, caught in these great currents. They moved majestically along their way regardless of the winds and tides on the surface.

I like this story because to me it's a wonderful example of the way a person should have his roots deep in a great, moving current—a moving stream of conscious direction—that will keep him on course, sailing steadily toward the destination he has chosen regardless of the economic and social winds that blow first this way and then that on the surface.

In such a life, there is no hurry, no frantic running about, no doubt or confusion. Instead, each day he moves a little way along his course—steadily, unrelentingly. In one day, he doesn't seem to make much headway to the casual observer, but, like the iceberg, if you come back in a week, you will no longer find him at the exact latitude and longitude of a week ago. And in a year, he will have covered a really marvelous distance, while most of those about him will still be moving in circles and by fits and starts. They'll go tearing past him one day like the hare sped by the turtle (if you don't mind my mixing my metaphors), but he plods steadily on, never looking back, thoroughly enjoying the trip. Above all, he has the wonderful calm knowledge of his destination and knows that each day finds him closing the distance that still separates him from it.

Sometimes in his life, as in all lives, there are storms that tend to throw him off course and obstacles that, for a time, may delay him. But soon, he's right back on course again, moving ahead.

This is the life of the strong, serene person—the person of wisdom. The person who knows that he cannot do or become everything in his lifetime calmly chooses that which he desires and which best fits his proclivity, pushes everything else from his mind, and begins his life's journey.

The life of such a man or woman always demonstrates the almost unbelievable cumulative effect of time well spent. His steady, unswerving use of time seems to make it compound until, in a very few years, he is miles ahead of all but the few who live as he does.

He's like the great iceberg: his roots are firmly held by the steady stream of his belief.

Ralph Waldo Emerson taught, "A point of education that I can never too much insist upon is this tenet that every individual man has a bias which he must obey, and that it is only as he feels and obeys this that he rightly develops and attains his legitimate power in the world."

Serendipity

THERE ARE FEW THINGS more interesting than words. Here's one you can add to your vocabulary and to your way of life, if you want to. The word is *serendipity*. The meaning of the word *serendipity*, according to the *Oxford Dictionary*, is "the faculty of making happy and unexpected discoveries by accident." And it means, also, the good things that almost always happen to a person following a bold course of action—serendipitous things.

The word was coined by a British author, Horace Walpole, who based it on the title of an old fairy tale, "The Three Princes of Serendip." The princes in the story were always making discoveries of things they were not in quest of.

Let's say you're trying to invent something. Frequently, you will stumble onto something entirely different—and wonderful—that you had no idea of discovering. That's what serendipity means. Now the point I want to make is that you wouldn't have made the serendipitous discovery if you hadn't been looking for something else.

I'll bet you've heard people say of someone, "That's the luckiest guy in the world." But if you'll get to know the man, you'll usually find he's a busy, positive kind of individual who's always looking for new and interesting ways of doing things. Someone once defined luck as something you find when preparedness meets opportunity. It just won't happen, usually, unless a person's prepared for it. There are lots of interesting and pretty wonderful things that would be happening all the time to a lot more people if people weren't such stick-in-the-muds, as a rule.

Take the person who hates his work, for example. There are millions of people, I suppose, who actually hate—loathe—the work they're doing. But they stay with it because of some warped sense of security. Now, if they'd find out what it is they'd really love to do and prepare themselves for it, they could cut loose of what they're doing now. The minute they did, this word *serendipity* would come into action—the good things that happen to a person following a bold, positive course of action.

It is frequently true that a lot of the boredom and frustration in a job comes from not knowing enough about it. You'd be surprised at the number of people who know only their own job—and that in a limited way—and who have no idea what's going on in the rest of the business. Frequently, a person in any given line of work can find interest, challenge, and just the job he's looking for, right in his own business or industry if he'd just take the time to find out more about it.

One of the greatest explorers who ever lived, Captain James Cook, began as an ordinary seaman. In four years, he had learned enough to become a master of his own ship and later made the discoveries that made him famous—a happy, successful, serendipitous life, beginning as a common seaman. Another common seaman, named Joseph Conrad, studied and worked his way to become a ship's captain. He later wrote the wonderful stories of the sea that made him loved and famous. There isn't a single line of work where this hasn't happened. I just picked a common seaman as an example. The same applies to anything.

Serendipity—quite a word. And it'll apply to whatever you do for a living.

Chapter Seven

The Practice of Being Human

Laughter: The Uniquely Human Cure

THERE'S A MARRIAGE COUNSELOR who has had a lot of success in saving marriages on the brink of dissolution by suggesting that whenever one of the partners starts an argument, the other partner should make him or her laugh. Real trouble begins when laughter goes out of a marriage.

One husband said, "How in the world can I get her to laugh? She hasn't laughed in three years."

"What made her laugh three years ago?" the counselor asked.

The husband thought for a moment and then said, "I fell on the ice in front of the house."

"Then you've got the answer. Whenever she starts an argument, fall down and make her laugh."

This made them both laugh, of course, and the doctor went on to suggest that the husband think of anything that might be silly enough to get them both laughing. "Stick celery in your ears... anything."

I remember many years ago we were rehearsing a dramatic radio series in Chicago, and the rehearsal had been going badly. The script wasn't the best; a couple of the actors and actresses weren't happy with their parts; the director was getting edgy; it was a cold, snowy day; and just as we were moodily about to try to do the dress rehearsal, since time was slipping away from us, one of the actors went out of the studio for a moment and returned suddenly with loud moans, staggering crazily, his eyes crossed and the ends of a pencil protruding from his ears. He had broken a long yellow pencil in half and had stuck the broken ends into his ears. Grisly as the sign was, appearing as it did that someone had pushed a pencil through his head, it threw us all—the director, the engineers, the sound effects people, and the musicians—into fits of uncontrolled laughter until we were helpless with tears running down our faces. From that point on we were all right, and the show was one of the best we did that year.

Laughter is wonderfully therapeutic. If your kids get into an argument, give them each a cloth or paper towel and put them on opposite sides of the same window with instructions to clean it. No matter how angry they may have been, just looking through the glass at each other cleaning the window will soon have them howling with laughter, the argument forgotten.

There was a doctor who made it a practice to look for pictures in magazines and newspapers of people laughing—laughing hard. He cut them out and pasted them in a scrapbook. When the book was full, he took it to the hospital and let the nurses pass it around the wards. You can't look at other people laughing without laughing yourself, and the effect on the patients and nurses was wonderful.

Perhaps this is why good comedians are among the highest paid of the world's performers: people need to laugh. You can't feel worried or depressed when you're convulsed with laughter. It seems to have a beneficial effect on the human mind and organs. We're the only creatures on earth who can laugh—and the only ones with enough problems to need it.

I remember reading about a husband who, when he had a nerve-wracking day at the office, would come home with his hat on backwards. If his wife had a bad day, she'd wear her apron backwards. In either case, it would start them laughing and clearing the air.

The Futility of Criticism

When we criticize another person, we set ourselves above him; we become the figure of authority and place the other person in an inferior position. The best rule to use when criticism springs to your mind is to wait.

I'VE GOT SOME ADVICE HERE for you today on how to become hated—how to stir up resentments and ill will that will simmer and hang on for years. All you have to do is...criticize!

No matter what a person has done, or how he lives his life, he doesn't want—nor does he feel he needs—criticism. This is why a criminal can fly into a rage against witnesses, prosecuting attorneys, and judges. Although he may have committed the most serious crime and knows full well that he has committed it, he deeply resents those who by their actions are critical of him.

The unfaithful husband or wife will, as often as not, fly into a wounded, self-pitying snit when confronted with evidence of his or her infidelity.

I'm not saying that people should not be criticized for criminal or moral misconduct. But I am saying that criticism makes a person try to justify himself, wounds his precious pride, hurts his sense of importance, and thoroughly arouses his resentment against the person or persons doing the criticizing.

When we criticize another person, we set ourselves above him; we become the figure of authority and place the other person in an inferior position. We automatically put the other person on the defensive. And even if he doesn't say anything and accepts the criticism meekly, it rankles.

When the husband at the bridge table says to his wife, "Well, my dear, you bid that hand like a certified moron," she might not say anything. She might not say anything at the moment, that is, but she's secretly praying for a miracle that will deliver a sawed-off shotgun into her hands. The other players squirm in embarrassment. And what does it accomplish? As Junius wrote, "It behooves the minor critic who hunts for blemishes to be a little distrustful of his own sagacity."

The best rule to use when criticism springs to your mind is to wait. Wait a while and try to look for the reasons behind the act you would criticize. It's also a good time ask oneself, "Who am I to be criticizing others? Am I really all that great and pure and all-knowing and perfect?" By all means wait until the heat of anger has dissipated. This is one of the world's most difficult things to do, and it takes a very mature person to master the wisdom and self-control to withhold criticism. But it's the way to greatness and one of the best known ways to earn the respect and/or love of others.

People know when they've done something wrong or foolish, and they usually know that you know it, too. And when you refrain from being critical, they're grateful; they respect you. As often as not, they'll be much tougher on themselves and make a concerted effort to avoid making the same mistake again. It's been said that the legitimate aim of criticism is to direct attention to the excellent. The bad will dig its own grave, and the imperfect may safely be left to that final neglect from which no amount of present undeserved popularity can rescue it.

As Epictetus put it, "Do not give sentence in another tribunal till you have been yourself judged in the tribunal of Justice." The key to overcoming the urge to criticize others is to wait. Wait a minute, or an hour, or a day...or forever.

Three Gifts to a Newborn Child

BILL BREWER was an especially astute interviewer and caught me completely off guard by his first question. He said, "If you could grant three qualities to a newborn child, what would they be?"

How would you like to be caught off guard early in the morning with that one? And for that matter, what would your answer be? "If you could grant three special qualities to a newborn child, what would they be?" I fed the question into my mental computer, thinking of my own children as I did, and I replied that I would grand the child, first, a consuming curiosity about everything—a love of knowledge. Second, I would grant the child a profound love for the earth and everything that lives upon it. And third, I would grant that child the gift of communication so that he or she could pass on to others what was learned during his or her lifetime.

Later, over breakfast, with more time to think about the question, I found I stuck with my original answers. How about you? What three gifts would you confer upon the child? Whatever they are, if your children are still young enough, or not yet born, you can pass them on to them.

With a love of learning, the person would never be bored nor find himself or herself stagnating at a certain level of accomplishment. The more we learn, the more we can do—and the more we venture to do, the more we learn. It's a self-generating perpetual motion kind of thing, for at least as long as we live. And with a deep love of learning, our person would develop a rich sense of humor, because as we learn more and more, the more we tend to pass through stultifying dogma and the lugubrious fearful threats preached by those who would keep us in bondage. Knowledge is freedom; freedom leads to joy and laughter. What was it Thucydides said? "The secret of happiness is freedom. And the secret of freedom is courage."

But with a love of the earth and all the living creatures on it, our person would have a deep sense of sympathy for anything or anyone in need. Our person would do whatever he or she could do to ameliorate suffering or the lack of personal freedom wherever it existed. Our person would be a natural champion of the environment but would understand that the environment is to be used and enjoyed as well as cared for and protected.

And as our person grew in maturity, he or she would most certainly be helping others to see the wonders and joys and problems of the world about us through one or more means of mass communication. Learning, loving, and communicating—not too bad, I should think. A lifetime of interest, love, and keeping in touch with life as we know it here on the planet Earth.

With those three qualities, our person would travel all over the earth and get to know this rather small speck of sand in the galaxy we call home and all the people and other living creatures that share it with us.

> **SUCCESS STARTS HERE**
>
> *What are some of the qualities you value in yourself that were passed on to you?*
>
> *What are the qualities you value in those closest to you?*
>
> *Are these qualities you possess or would like to possess? How would they improve your life?*

Chapter Eight

Some of Life's Lessons

The Tale of the Butterfly

THERE'S A STORY ATTRIBUTED TO Henry Miller, the writer, about a little boy in India who walks up to a guru—an Indian wise man—who is sitting and looking at something in his hand. The little boy goes up and looks at it. He doesn't quite understand what it is so he says to the guru, "What is that?"

"It's a cocoon," the guru tells him. "Inside the cocoon is a butterfly. Soon the cocoon is going to split, and the butterfly will come out."

"Could I have it?" asks the little boy.

"Yes," says the guru, "but you must promise me that when the cocoon splits, and the butterfly starts to come out, and he is beating his wings to get out of the cocoon, you won't help him. Don't help the butterfly by breaking the cocoon apart. Let him do it by himself."

The little boy promised, took the cocoon, went home with it, and then sat and watched it. Finally, he saw it begin to vibrate and move and quiver, and finally the cocoon split. Inside was a beautiful damp butterfly, frantically beating its wings against the cocoon, trying to get out and not seeming to be able to do it. The little boy desperately wanted to help. Finally, he gave in and disobeyed the guru's orders. He pushed the two halves of the cocoon apart, and the butterfly sprang out. But, as soon as it got up in the air, it fell down to the ground and was killed. The little boy picked up the dead butterfly and in tears went back to the guru and showed it to him.

"You see, little boy," the guru said, "you pushed open the cocoon, didn't you?"

"Yes," said the little boy.

And the guru said, "You don't understand. You didn't see what you were doing. When the butterfly comes out of the cocoon, the only way he can strengthen his wings is by beating them against the cocoon. It beats against the cocoon so its muscles will grow. When you helped it the way you did, you prevented it from getting strong. That's why the butterfly fell to the ground and was killed."

It's a story every parent should remember...and perhaps pass along to the youngsters when they're old enough to understand. Handing a child a toy he wants instead of letting him crawl across the room for it or try his best to crawl for it; fulfilling his every whim; loading him down with the shiny, beautiful things of our society before he really needs or desires them; talking about the importance of grades in school instead of the importance of education—all of these things tend to weaken the muscles he should be developing on his own so that when the time comes for him to fly, he will have the strength he needs.

It's a good story to tell at the dinner table and to discuss. So often what seems harsh or cruel in nature is in reality wisdom and kindness for the time ahead.

To Whom We Owe the Most

I REMEMBER READING SOMEWHERE that we owe the most to those people who make us become what we can become. Whatever little knowledge we have acquired has been because of the knowledge, thoughts, and ideas that others before us have managed to piece together. We have taken them as our foundation and have built upon them.

That has not been an unbroken upward movement by any means. There have been times in our history when the light has all but gone out for hundreds of years, and it could happen again. But we owe an incalculable debt to those tireless thinkers and researchers who have added increments of new information to the growing store of total knowledge.

There are those who say, "Why bother with continuing education, continuing to study? Why learn all that, go to all that work and bother, just to carry it to the grave?" But that isn't the way it works. We don't carry it to the grave; we pass it along—and often in a new and more enlightened form, sometimes even with a brand-new idea that brightens the pathway ahead for those who follow.

I'm sure we don't do it for such noble purposes. We do it, I suppose, because we're curious, because it seems to be a part of us to want to know—to want to know all we can know during our brief turn at life. There is excitement in coming upon new information. It is for the seeker after knowledge what a gold strike is for the prospector. He wants to throw his hat in the air and dance for joy. "Look what I've found," he says as he passes it along to his family, his classroom, his readers. And so they find it, too; they can enjoy and use it, too, and in their turn pass it along.

And one of them will take the new knowledge and, using it like a piece in a jigsaw puzzle, fit it into a larger picture so that it contributes to a wholly new idea—an idea that would have been incomplete and impossible without it. And then that new idea contributes to another, and so on, so that new pictures—bigger pictures—continue to emerge.

From time to time there are setbacks. Ideas are not always good in the form in which they're produced. The discovery of dynamite by Nobel was a boon to the construction industry, but it was also a new boom to the sound of war.

We developed thinking, as birds developed wings, in order to survive in a hostile environment. Weak and vulnerable in a world of savage beasts with the need to survive against competition more formidably armed than himself, we turned to the cerebral cortex, the thin layer of gray matter that covered the rudimentary brain, and it responded. It responded so astonishingly that we were able to build a shuttle system to the moon and harness the power and heat of the sun. And it is still responding, growing every day more complex. Most of us never use 20 percent of our thinking equipment. Some say most idle along at 5 percent.

If most people realized the fun and profit to be gained from a systematic prospecting of their minds, they would devote an hour or so a day to it—maybe more. But most don't know about it and seldom think from one year to the next.

After You Know It All

Individuals who remain vital have learned not to be imprisoned by fixed habits, attitudes, and routines. We build our own prisons and serve as our own jailers. But if we build the prisons ourselves, we can tear them down ourselves. If we are willing to learn, the opportunities are everywhere.

I RECEIVED A LETTER FROM Douglas Stovall in Danville, Virginia, with a copy of a short piece by John W. Gardner that I had never seen before. It's called "The Things You Learn after You Know It All." I found it excellent. See what you think of it.

"Would you bet on the future of this man? He is 53 years old. Most of his adult life has been a losing struggle against debt and misfortune. A war injury has denied him the use of his left hand. He's had several jobs, succeeded at none, and has often been to prison. Driven by heaven knows what motives—boredom, hope of gain, creative impulse—he determines to write a book. The book turns out to be one that has enthralled the world for more than 350 years. The former prisoner was Cervantes, and the book was *Don Quixote*." And the story poses an interesting question: "Why do some men and women discover new vitality and creativity to the end of their days, while others go to seed long before?"

We've all known people who run out of steam before they reach life's halfway mark. I'm talking about the people who have stopped learning or growing because they've adopted the fixed attitudes and opinions that all too often come with passing years. Most of us, in fact, progressively narrow the scope and variety of our lives. We succeed in our field of specialization and then become trapped in it. Nothing surprises us. We lose our sense of wonder and adventure.

But if you're conscious of these dangers, you can resort to countervailing measures. Reject stagnation. Reject the myth that learning is for young people. It's what you learn after you know it all that counts.

Learn all your life from your successes and failures. When you hit a spell of trouble, ask, "What is it trying to teach me?" The lessons aren't always happy ones. In one of his essays, Ralph Waldo Emerson wrote, "Bad times have a scientific value. These are occasions a good learner would not miss."

Individuals who remain vital have learned not to be imprisoned by fixed habits, attitudes, and routines. We build our own prisons and serve as our own jailers. But if we build the prisons ourselves, we can tear them down ourselves. If we are willing to learn, the opportunities are everywhere. We learn from our work and from our friends and families. We learn by accepting the obligations of

Some of Life's Lessons

life, by suffering, by taking risks, by loving, by bearing life's indignities with dignity.

The things you learn in maturity seldom involve information and skills. You learn to bear the things you can't change. You learn to avoid self-pity. You learn not to burn up energy in anxiety. You learn that most people are neither for nor against you but rather are thinking about themselves. You learn that no matter how much you try to please, some people are never going to love you—a notion that troubles at first but is eventually relaxing.

Among your obligations is an appointment with yourself. Self-knowledge, the beginning of wisdom, is ruled out for most people by the increasingly effective self-deception they practice as they grow older. By middle age, most of us are accomplished fugitives from ourselves. Yet there's a surprising usefulness in learning not to lie to yourself.

One of the most valuable things you learn is that ultimately you're the one who's responsible for you. You don't blame others. You don't blame circumstances. You take charge. If you're going to keep on learning, your surest allies will be high motivation and enthusiasm.

YOUR SUCCESS STARTS HERE

Doing What You Love to Do

MANY YEARS AGO, there was a very successful executive in a financial concern. He was getting along in years when he finally decided he didn't like the work he was in. It was all right—he was successful at it because he was intelligent and hard-working—but it wasn't what he really wanted to do.

This particular executive happened to be interested in birds. He wanted to become an expert on birds—an ornithologist. So, in his spare time, he began his studies. He read every book he could find that had anything to do with birds. He studied so steadily that before he knew it, he was writing books about birds himself and helping out with the bird displays at the museum. His name was Dr. Frank Chapman. He became curator of ornithology at the American Museum of Natural History. He was doing something he wanted to do—really enjoyed doing—and he was well along in years before he made the decision that gave new direction, meaning, and happiness to his life.

The point I want to make is that it's almost never too late to change to work you really enjoy. It's happened hundreds of times that men and women have retired at sixty-five with the security of a pension and have turned to the field they should have been in all along. They have accomplished more in five years in the work they love than they had in the forty years with their previous companies.

So, here's some unasked-for advice if you happen to be in work you don't particularly enjoy: First, find out what you'd really like to do. Determine your objective and actually visualize it in your mind. Picture what you want and the kind of person you want to become.

Next, get the facts. Get all the facts about what will be required to attain the objective you've determined upon and visualized. The more information you can get on the subject, the better.

Next, analyze, evaluate, and group those facts. Try to put them in the logical order of importance of accomplishment. For example, if a person wanted to become a brain surgeon, she wouldn't just start opening up heads; she'd start with school. Make sure your goal is practical for you.

Then set a timetable for the accomplishment of your objectives and try to stick to the timetable. Don't let people throw you off-track or tell you that you're wrong. You should know what's right for you. What's right for others is their business.

Next, begin! Don't just keep talking about it. Do it! And understand that the time will really never be perfect to start, so start as soon as you're ready. You'll never get to second base trying to keep one foot on first. Take off! If you're tagged out, you can come to bat again.

Be sure your entire plan is written out—a regular blueprint to follow—and you can check, from time to time, to see how you're doing by comparing your progress with your blueprint.

And finally, stay with it. Keep your goal firmly fixed in your mind, have faith that you can reach it—and reach it, you will. And like Dr. Frank Chapman, you'll find yourself happy and excited in work you really enjoy.

What is more important than spending our lives in work we really enjoy? Yet there are millions who don't know it's possible, who largely waste their lives. It's a shame, isn't it?

Chapter Nine

Thoughts on Existence

Reminders of Mortality

Back in the days of ancient Rome, during the years of the Caesars, there was a person whose only job was to hold a laurel wreath over the head of Caesar and from time to time intone the words, "Thou art mortal."

The purpose of this was to remind the man in whom such great powers resided that he, too, was, after all, only a man and, as such, mortal.

When we're young, we tend to think of life as never-ending. Time, for us, stretches off limitlessly into the future. but as we get older, even into our forties—which should be a time of vigor, interest, and activity; really, a time of young maturity—we begin to get, from time to time, small reminders of our mortality. It might be a sudden shortness of breath or a perfectly normal twinge in the chest...a bit of back trouble. But we get these occasional reminders that time is not, after all, standing still for us; that we, like the Caesars of old, are indeed mortal.

To the neurotic, this sort of reminder fills him with dread and plunges him into even deeper depression. But to the fairly normal, reasonably well-adjusted person, this comes as a reminder to enjoy to the fullest the time that is remaining; that days are not things to be waited through until Saturday, or a birthday, or Christmas, but rather to be savored and enjoyed one by one, hour by hour. We come to an understanding that to "kill time," as we so aptly put it, is really nothing more than to kill a little part of ourselves, since time is all we have.

It reminds us, too (or at least it should) to be more patient, more tolerant of others, particularly those we love. If we're mature enough to love everyone, it means exactly that. And it reminds us to follow our hunches and obey our sudden impulses, especially those that involve a kind word, or a pat on the back, or a sign of tenderness. Those we love, as well as ourselves, are only passengers for the journey's duration. Let's let them know we enjoy sharing it with them. And if we don't always enjoy it, let's fake it; let's pretend we do. After all, the trip really isn't all that long.

I saw a newspaper picture not long ago of a woman seventy-five years old who was ice skating. It reminded me that seventy-five is only old to people under sixty years of age. To people who are seventy-five, it's a good, thoroughly enjoyable age. And maybe we'll all live to be eighty-five or ninety-five, and maybe we won't. In any case, there is a limit, and there should be or it wouldn't be there. And since there is, why not relax a little? Don't take things too seriously. And as an old friend of mine once said, "In a life where death is inevitable, never worry about anything!"

Sure, it's easier said than done. I remember reading a story about an old man who was planting a young tree in his yard. His neighbor hailed him and said, "What are you planting the tree for? You'll never live to see it grown." And the old man calmly went on with his planting and said, "I believe you have to plan on dying tomorrow or living forever. I'm not planning on dying tomorrow."

Yes, the smart people of the world—the really mature people—are those who know the length of the journey is limited. They don't dwell on this. But they make certain they enjoy every day of the trip as much as they possibly can.

Enjoy the Interval

GEORGE SANTAYANA once wrote, "There is no cure for birth and death save to enjoy the interval." It's being reminded of something like this that can really shake a person.

Have you ever thought about how much time we waste and unhappiness we bring upon ourselves by worrying about the future and reliving in our minds the mistakes of the past?

One of the neatest tricks in the world is to learn to enjoy the present, since the present is the only time we will ever own. Distance is no longer a serious obstacle due to modern means of travel, but time remains unconquerable. It cannot be expanded, accumulated, mortgaged, hastened, or retarded. It is the one thing completely beyond man's control. And while the supply of time is certainly limited for anyone, generally it is squandered as though there is no end to it.

The man on the commuter train, bored, waiting to get home, then waiting for dinner, then waiting to go to bed or for a particular television program, thus spends his time slightly behind reality, waiting for something that's coming up. And while it will keep him going, he never, or seldom, learns to enjoy the time he is using right now. What it takes is an awareness of living. It means being aware that you are alive at this moment and that the world and people are interesting enough at any time that we need not waste so precious a thing as time in boredom.

If we know where we're going in the future, we can do our work to the best of our ability, give it everything we have, and have no need to worry about it or the future. And as for reliving our mistakes of the past, this is the easiest advice on earth to give and probably the most difficult to follow. Everybody knows it's perfectly useless to relive in our minds the foolish stunts we've pulled in the past, but this doesn't keep us from doing it. Again, according to the experts, the solution may be found in living for the present and enjoying it as much as we can. This does not mean that we should not plan for the future. We should! But once our plans are laid, work on them, but don't stew and fret over them.

All we will ever have is today. Yesterday is gone forever; it can never be recalled. And tomorrow never comes. If we find it difficult to enjoy the day in which we're living, we should remember that what we're waiting for will be made up of the same kind of days we're getting now.

Frequently, a person who is unhappy by nature will believe that when something happens in the future such as marriage, a better job, more money, or whatever it happens to be, he will suddenly be a happy person. The facts don't bear that out. If we're living in the past, or worrying, or hoping for happiness in the future, the best thing we can do is ask ourselves, "How am I doing with the days I'm getting right now? How am I doing today? It is not how much we have but how much we enjoy that makes happiness. Try the business of being aware of the present and its possibilities, and chances are you'll enjoy it.

The Greatest Gift on Earth

Millions of people with the miracle of sight never really see the world about them until it's practically too late. Millions with the inborn capacity to love and to know the joy that loving brings wait too long to express it.

IN INTERVIEWS WITH very old people—people who realize that their remaining time is drawing to a close—you frequently hear them say, "I waited too long to start living."

When the researchers, or others who hear this kind of response, are young, they find it strange. But what these older people mean is that they often failed to enjoy life even during the years that they were living it most fully. And it seems that most people, during the richest and fullest years of their lives, fail to develop an awareness of living, an enjoyment of living.

It's like the person who puts the best china and silver and linen away for some future or very special time and dies before any of it is ever used. Or it's like the person who puts seat covers in his car and thus passes on to the second person to buy it brand-new upholstery that he himself never used or enjoyed.

And so, millions of people with the miracle of sight never really see the world about them until it's practically too late. Millions with the inborn capacity to love and to know the joy that loving brings wait too long to express it. They live through the passing years without really being aware of their days, of the riches that are passing through their hands.

Few people, it seems, develop an awareness of daily living. In possession of the miracle of life, they pass through their days like automatons. In possession of the greatest gift on earth—life itself—they tell us by their actions that they don't even know they have it and haven't the slightest conception of its value, let alone an awareness that it is to be enjoyed to the fullest every day.

I remember reading an account of a famous show-business personality—a woman of great talent—who, as she made the announcement of her impending fourth or fifth marriage, said, "After all these years, I am finally going to be happy." She thought another husband could somehow give her something she should have been enjoying all along. She obviously had no idea as to what happiness is, where it's to be found, or what living is all about. And she belongs to a big club.

It is only when life is threatened that a conception of its value begins to dawn on the average person.

A man plotted a kidnapping for months. His mind was filled with the thought of the million-dollar ransom he was going to get—more important to him, he thought at the time, than anything else on earth. Yet when he was surprised by the police, he dropped the suitcase containing the ransom and ran for dear life. It took the sudden threat of death to put things in their proper order for this poor, stupid person.

It's amazing, isn't it? Most people place the greatest value on the cheapest things in life, while the greatest gift of all—life itself—goes unnoticed.

The most fortunate people in the world are those who have the wisdom to place value where it belongs—those who have an awareness of life.

It Alone Is Life

SOME 4,500 YEARS AGO, one of the most inspiring thoughts the world has ever produced was written in Sanskrit. Here's its translation: "Look well to this one day, for it and it alone is life. In the brief course of this one day lie all the verities and realities of your existence: the pride of growth, the glory of action, the splendor of beauty. Yesterday is only a dream, and tomorrow is but a vision. Yet each day, well lived, makes every yesterday a dream of happiness and each tomorrow a vision of hope. Look well, therefore, to this one day, for it and it alone is life."

With that one bit of ancient philosophy and little else, a person could live an ideal and richly successful life. It applies to everyone in every walk of life—certainly the student, the teacher, the businessperson, the worker (whatever his or her task may be), the housewife, the politician, the clergyman.

I remember reading somewhere about a businessman who visits his barbershop every morning for a half hour. He doesn't want a shave or haircut. He lies stretched out in the chair with a hot towel on his face, not just because it is soothing and relaxing, but so no one will recognize and speak to him. And during that half hour, he gets himself organized mentally for the day ahead. It sounds like a good idea. But I think everyone could accomplish much the same thing by sitting quietly and slowly reading that great piece of Sanskrit wisdom.

"Look well to this one day, for it and it alone is life." It's true.

Today, right now, is all the life there is for any person on earth. We can look toward and plan for the future, certainly. But if we pass up living and enjoying today, we're passing up all we've got for something we hope to get.

"In the brief course of this one day lie all the verities and realities of your existence: the pride of growth, the glory of action, the splendor of beauty." In reading and thinking of this at the beginning of each new day, we would remind ourselves of these points: the truth and reality of our lives, in themselves a miracle. And we would remind ourselves of our duty to grow a little as persons, to rise above the petty and the trivial, to become stronger and more serene. And we would remind ourselves to take some action calculated to move us a notch closer to our goals and toward fulfillment as persons and to recognize and be aware of the beauty around us.

The proof of the greatness and truth of this piece of writing is in the fact that it has successfully withstood the test of time and has endured for more than 4,500 years. It is as modern and important today as it was the day it first flashed across the mind of some person whose name has long been forgotten. And it will be just as important to thinking men and women 4,500 years from today, for real truth is as ageless as the mountains, as enduring as the sea.

The Wish to Be Like Someone Else

When a person finds himself, when he stops imitating and envying others, there is something in his nature that says to him, "This is it. You've found your road at last."

RALPH WALDO EMERSON wrote, "There is a time in every man's education when he arrives at the conviction that envy is ignorance, that imitation is suicide, that he must take himself for better or worse as his portion; that though the wide universe is full of good, no kernel of nourishing corn can come to him but through the toil bestowed on that plot of ground which is given him to till. The power which resides in him is new in nature, and none but he knows what that is which he can do, nor does he know until he has tried.... Trust thyself: Every heart vibrates to that iron string."

There is a bit of advice that a person would do well to reflect upon every morning of his life. No one can even estimate the number of people who live nervous, anxious, unhappy lives because they daily attempt the impossible, which is to be like someone else. They are people who don't realize the truth of Emerson's words—that envy is ignorance, that imitation is suicide. He must have used the word *suicide* because we have to kill that which is natural in our selves when we attempt to be like someone else.

They need to recognize the truth, also, that the power that resides in them is new in nature, that it has never appeared before, in just that way, on earth; that if they'll learn about and develop their own powers, they'll have no need of envy or imitation.

Envy is ignorance because it means a person is ignorant of his own powers and abilities, his one-of-a-kind natural talent. He has never looked within himself for his own road to greatness but instead seeks it in the lives of others. And when he fails to succeed as do those he envies—and fail he must, because he cannot possibly be exactly like them—his image of himself shrinks. Not understanding that he is unlike those he envies, he does not realize that this simple fact lies at the bottom of his failure. Nor does he understand that he can be as successful as anyone on earth if he will build upon that power that resides in him.

As Emerson put it, "The power which resides in him is new in nature, and none but he knows what that is which he can do, nor does he know until he has tried."

This is why a parent is off-base when he says to a child, "Why aren't you like so-and-so? Look at what he's doing." The parent doesn't understand that it's a human impossibility for the child to be like so-and-so and to do what he does in the same way.

Instead, a parent would be wise to say, "Don't worry about so-and-so. He's found his strength, and he's building on it. You have strength of your own, and when you find it, you can build just as high."

And then those great words: "Trust thyself: Every heart vibrates to that iron string." When a person finds himself, when he stops imitating and envying others, there is something in his nature that says to him, "This is it. You've found your road at last."

Every person is born to be a star at something. The purpose of his life is to discover it and then to spend his years building upon that plot of ground it was given to him to till.

The Identity Trap

WHAT MAKES YOU HAPPY will depend on your own personal nature, which is different in many ways from that of any other human being. To try to find happiness by doing what seems to make others happy is to fall head first into the identity trap. So writes Harry Browne in his book *How I Found Freedom in an Unfree World*.

He believes that there are two identity traps: (1) the belief that you should be someone other than yourself and (2) the assumption that others will do things in the way that you would. These are the basic traps, of which many others are variations. In the first trap, you necessarily forfeit your freedom by requiring yourself to live in a stereotyped, predetermined way that doesn't consider your own desires, feelings, and objectives.

The second trap is more subtle but just as harmful to your freedom. When you expect someone to have the same ideas, attitudes, and feelings that you have, you expect him or her to act in ways that aren't in keeping with his or her nature. As a result, you'll expect and hope that people will do things they're not capable of doing.

Others can suggest what you "should" do or what "ought" to make you happy, but they will often be wrong. You have to determine for yourself who you are, what makes you happy, what you're capable of doing, and what you want to do. Be open to suggestions, but never forfeit the power to make the final decision yourself. Only then can you act in ways that will bring you happiness.

You're in the identity trap when you let others determine what's right or wrong for you—when you live by unquestioned rules that define how you should act and think.

You're in the identity trap, says Mr. Browne, when you try to be interested in something because it's expected of you, or when you try to do the things that others have said you should do, or when you try to live up to an image that others say is the only legitimate, valid image you're allowed to have.

You're in the identity trap if you allow others to define labels and impose them upon you—such as going to PTA meetings because that's what a so-called "good parent" is supposed to do, or going to visit your parents every Sunday because a "good child" would never do less, or giving up your career because a so-called "good wife" puts her husband's career first.

You're in the identity trap if you feign an interest in ecology to prove your civic interest, or give to the poor to prove you aren't selfish, or study dull subjects to appear to be "intellectual."

You're in the identity trap if you buy an expensive car to prove you're successful or a small foreign car because your friends are anti-Detroit; or if you shave every day to prove you're respectable or let your hair grow long to prove you don't conform. In any of these ways, you allow someone else to determine what you should think and be. You deny your own self when you suppress desires that aren't considered "legitimate," or when you try to appear to be having fun because everyone else is, or when you settle for a certain life because you've been told that's all you should expect in the world.

The Power of Reason

MOST OF THE EARTH'S CREATURES have been given the gift of concealment through protective coloring. In fact, all of them that need concealment blend in so well with their natural surroundings that when they're motionless, they become virtually invisible. This, of course, protects them from the sight of their enemies or their quarry. They, through the endless ages of evolution, have conformed to their environment; they have copied the appearance of their natural surroundings.

But what of man? He is among the weakest, physically, of all creatures. He can be killed by a leopard that is one-fourth his weight or by a germ or virus that's totally invisible. He has no protective coloring at all but can easily be seen in any kind of environment. He can't run fast enough to escape any animal bent on catching him. He can't swim very far. He has no claws or sharp teeth and can hardly climb a tree. His vision is weak, and he can't even catch a puppy that doesn't want to be caught.

But he was given the greatest gift of all—reason! He can think. Because he can think, he doesn't need to blend in with his surroundings, his environment. He can make his surroundings and environment change to match him. In fact, just as you can tell what kind of country an animal comes from by looking at the pattern of its coloring, you can tell what kind of reasoning a person is doing by observing his surroundings, his environment, because environment fits the person, just as an animal fits its environment.

To the exact extent that a person uses the greatest gift on earth, the gift of reasoning, of thinking—which belongs to him alone of all the creatures on earth—will determine the kind of environment in which he will live. Only man can make the scenery change to match him.

By changing himself, he changes his surroundings. If a person understands this, he understands, at the same time, why he is king over everything else. Because of this, he solves the riddles of the invisible germs, travels with the speed of two hundred hurricanes, swims to the bottom of the sea, and will one day visit the farthest planets of the universe.

And yet, it is here we find the greatest paradox: with this greatest gift of all, the great majority of people neither know they have it, nor use it, but spend most of their time aping those about them—playing a silly kind of copycat game that you'd expect to see in a tribe of baboons cavorting on the forest floor. No two of them are exactly alike, and yet they pretend they are; and they let a handful of their brothers do their thinking for them. Each of them has been given the greatest gift on earth, and he doesn't even open the box.

I think from time to time it would be good for all of us to remember Archibald MacLeish's great line: "The only thing about a man that is a man...is his mind. Everything else you can find in a pig or a horse."

The Lives We Imagine

HERE'S SOMETHING WORTH keeping in mind: "If one advances confidently in the direction of his dreams and endeavors to live the life which he has imagined, he will meet with a success unexpected in common hours." It was written by Henry David Thoreau. And it contains a truth most people do not even dream exists. If they did, the entire country might be turned into total chaos.

The truth most of us miss in that great quotation is that success—beyond anything we might now imagine—lies in wait for those who can put together enough courage to actually live the life they imagine.

Most people live in two worlds: there's the real world, the world in which they move and work and live, the world of the nitty-gritty; and there's the world of the imagination, the world in which they would secretly like to live. And what keeps them from moving from the world of reality into the world of their imagination is habit and the fear of falling flat on their faces in the attempt, and losing even the little that they presently have, and perhaps looking ridiculous in the eyes of their loved ones and friends. They are like the character Walter Mitty, created by James Thurber. They are the people who dream their whole lives instead of living their dreams. We're all Walter Mittys to some extent.

What we fail to realize is what Thoreau discovered—that if one advances confidently in the direction of his dreams and endeavors to live the life that he has imagined, he will meet with a success unexpected in common hours.

Thoreau knew this because he did it. So have thousands of others who have found, to their delighted surprise, that life pays off most handsomely when we are doing that which we most want to do, when we are actually living the life we have imagined for so long.

That doesn't mean that we run off after every vagrant whim. But it does mean that we should live the life that we know deep down in our very being we would most like to live. It means that we should be doing that which every indicator of our makeup, every fiber of our being, tells us we should be doing…and has been telling us for some time. Even Thoreau didn't go to live at Walden Pond the first time the idea struck him to go off by himself and meditate and think and write and try to discover for himself what was important and what wasn't.

But when an idea tugs at us day after day, year after year; when we think about it as we lie awake in bed or the first thing when we wake up; when it worries our consciousness like a puppy with a slipper, then it's time to do something about it. And even though making the move might seem to jeopardize everything of order in our lives, it is very likely, as Thoreau suggested, that we will meet with a success unexpected in common hours. The most commonly voiced thought after taking such a step is, "Why didn't I do this years ago?"

Emerson said, "A man should learn to detect and watch that gleam of light which flashes across his mind from within more than the luster of the firmament of bards and sages. Yet he dismisses without notice his thought because it is his."

> ## SUCCESS STARTS HERE
>
> **When was the last time you allowed yourself to nurture your imagination?**
>
> **Do you take the time to write down your dreams and thoughts?**
>
> **If the idea of taking a big risk to pursue your dreams frightens you, consider taking small steps first and watch your success grow!**

The Man, the Seashore, and the Four Prescriptions

ONCE UPON A TIME, there was a man who felt he'd reached the end of his rope. It seemed that all the interest had suddenly vanished from his life; his creative wells had seemingly dried up. He still had his work, but it suddenly seemed meaningless to him. Even his family and his home receded darkly in his mind.

Finally, nearing the point of desperation, he went to see his old friend, the family doctor. The doctor listened to his story, saw the depth of his depression, and then asked him, "When you were a child, what did you like to do best?"

"I liked to visit the seashore," he said.

"Alright," the doctor said, "you must do exactly as I tell you. I want you to spend all day tomorrow at the shore. Find a lonely stretch of beach and spend the entire day there from nine o'clock in the morning until six o'clock in the evening. Take nothing to read, and do nothing calculated to distract you in any way. I'm going to give you four prescriptions in order. Take the first at nine o'clock, the second at noon, the third at three o'clock, and the last at six o'clock. Don't look at them now. Wait until you arrive at the shore tomorrow morning."

The man promised he would take the doctor's advice, and the next morning, a little before nine o'clock, he parked his car on a lonely stretch of beach. There was a strong wind blowing in from the sea, and the surf was high and pounding.

He walked to a sand dune near the seething surf and sat down. He took out prescription number one, opened it, and read it. It said, "Listen!" That was all that was written on it—the one word: "Listen!" And so for three hours, that's all he did. He listened to the sound of the buffeting wind and the lonely cries of the gulls. He listened to the sound of the booming surf. He sat quietly, and he listened.

At noon, he read the second prescription. It said simply, "Reach back." And so for the next three hours, he did just that. He let his mind go back as far as it could go, and he thought of all the incidents of his life he could remember—the happy times, the good times, the struggles, and the successes.

At three o'clock, he tore open the third prescription. It read, "Re-examine your motives." And this took so much intense thought and concentration that the remaining three hours slipped quickly by. For three hours, he re-examined his motives, his reasons for living, and moved closer to fulfillment. He clarified and restated his goals.

And at six o'clock, under a gray, darkening sky and with a taste of salt spray on the wind, he read the fourth and final prescription. It read, "Write your worries in the sand."

There had been one thing that had been worrying him particularly, so he walked to the hard sand and, with a stick, wrote this worry in the sand and stood looking at it for a moment. Then, as he walked toward where his car was parked, he looked back and saw that the incoming tide had already erased his worry. He got in his car and drove homeward.

My old friend, Norman Vincent Peale, told me that story some years back about the man, the seashore, and the four prescriptions:

listen, reach back, re-examine your motives, and then write your worries in the sand.

Life Comes Full Circle

THE HEAD OF A GREAT CORPORATION died in his New York office of a heart attack. Later, when it came time to clean out his desk and collect his personal effects, a hand fishing line, wrapped on a stick, complete with bobber, sinker, and hook, was found in his bottom desk drawer. It was probably the one he had used as a small boy on the family farm in the Midwest.

Had that relic of younger, carefree days represented his real dream of what living was all about?

He had gone to school, found a job, got married, worked hard, purchased a home on the installment plan, and won the other niceties of living. Children had come along, and there was their education to think about. There were promotions that had come from hard work and native ability and the passing of the years. There were the clubs and civic things, the professional associates, the crises on the job and at home, and finally the top job with a company that had grown very much larger with the passing of thirty years—the top job, with its responsibilities to stockholders, employees, customers, research and development, and finance. The kids were out of school and married now. It had all happened so fast and with no real plan of any kind. It had been school, then job, then work, then promotions, and family, and income problems, and suddenly there he was, on top of the pile.

And rummaging in his things in the attic or the basement one day, he had come across that old, worn-out fishing outfit, with its tiny hook for bluegills and the red bobber with the paint all peeled off. The string had almost come apart in his hands. And he had sat there and remembered that cool little creek with the summer smell of it, the green moss along the bank, the frogs plopping into the water, the water bugs skimming, and the willows along the bank. He remembered the excitement of seeing that bobber suddenly disappear, and the frantic tug of the fish on the line, and finally a nice string of them for dinner.

And suddenly he had wanted to go back. He had realized that that had been living—that had been real, and elemental, and satisfying. And somehow, he hadn't done enough of it. He hadn't had the time to just go sit on a bank, and fish for a while, and chew on a twig, and feel the sun on his back, and wait for the bobber to disappear; the time and the leisure to listen to the voice inside and get things straightened out in his mind as to what was important and what wasn't—things like goals and roles.

So someone had called him, and he'd put the fishing outfit in his jacket pocket. And he thought about it the next morning, too, when he took the outfit to the office and looked at it again and then finally put it down in that bottom drawer—out of sight, but not out of mind. And then there'd been the coronary, and that had been the end of that. The fishing outfit was still in the bottom drawer. And when his wife went through the effects they sent home from his office, she sat with the fishing outfit in her hand for a long time. She saw him as a little boy, too, and wondered why he had followed the course he'd chosen.

Mentoring

WE LIVE BY EXAMPLE. As youngsters, our parents set our example. As we grow older, examples are set for us by our parents and the people with whom we habitually associate—relatives, the friends of our family, our neighbors—and the school we attend.

We take our cues from those about us. It's all we can do. We are born not knowing how to survive in the world. We must learn how over a period of many years. So we watch and we listen to those about us, and we conduct ourselves as they do. What they take for granted as part of living we learn to take for granted. We devote seventeen, perhaps eighteen years or more to living at home with people who are, in every sense of the word, our teachers. And the quality of our lives and our learning will, of course, depend on the quality of their habit-knit, automatic response to living. We live and learn by example.

Peter Drucker wrote, "The best prescription for achievement is to have an achieving father or mother—better yet, an achieving milieu." High achievement seldom accrues to a man or woman who has not been inspired by a mentor. The word *mentor* means "wise and trusted counselor." This counselor can be a schoolteacher, a manager, a friend—anyone who represents what we most want to become.

The *Harvard Business Review* said that "everyone who makes it has a mentor." And Lee Iacocca said, "You've got to have mentors along the way."

If every young person could have a wise and trusted counselor to lead him step by step onto the wise and rewarding pathways of the world, all would be well.

My old friend, the late Eric Hoffer, said, "Those who invest themselves in becoming all they can become—and, more important than that, those who invest themselves in helping others become all they can become—are involved in the most important work on the face of the earth. That is, they are helping to complete God's plan."

We should never forget that we are setting an example for others—example is the school of mankind—and that the flame of a candle is not diminished when it is used to light another. Consider, for example, what is believed to have been the greatest intellectual succession in history: Socrates was the teacher of Plato; Plato, in turn, was the teacher of Alexander the Great. We might not have had the great works of Plato had it not been for Socrates and his questioning method of teaching. And the only reason we know anything about Socrates is because Plato wrote down his words. Socrates never wrote down anything at all.

As adults, we tend to be mentors—or, at least, an example—to others as well as protégées of the person or persons who managed us and who set examples for us.

SUCCESS STARTS HERE

Can you think of someone who is your mentor?

Are you in some ways patterning your life after this individual?

If you became exactly like your mentor, would you be content?

Do you feel you can transcend—go beyond—your mentor to reach new levels?

Earl Nightingale's Biography

As a Depression-era child, Earl Nightingale was hungry for knowledge. From the time he was a young boy, he would frequent the Long Beach Public Library in New York, searching for the answer to the question, "How can a person, starting from scratch, who has no particular advantage in the world, reach the goals that he feels are important to him, and by so doing, make a major contribution to others?" His desire to find an answer, coupled with his natural curiosity about the world and its workings, spurred him to become one of the world's foremost experts on success and what makes people successful.

His early career began when, as a member of the Marine Corps, he volunteered to work at a local radio station as an announcer, sharing some of the ideas he had uncovered during his inquisitive youth. The Marines also give him his first chance to travel, although he only got as far as Hawaii when the Japanese attacked Pearl Harbor in 1941. Earl managed to be one of the few survivors aboard the battleship *Arizona*. After five more years in the service, Earl and his wife moved first to Phoenix, then to Chicago, to build what was to be a very fruitful career in network radio. As the host of his own daily commentary program on WGN, Earl arranged a deal that also gave him a commission on his own advertising sales. By 1957, he was so successful he decided to retire at the age of thirty-five.

In the meantime, he had bought his own insurance company and had spent many hours motivating its sales force to greater profits. When he decided to go on vacation for an extended period of time, his sales manager begged him to put his inspirational words on record. The result later became the recording entitled *The Strangest Secret*, the first spoken word message to win a Gold Record by selling over a million copies. About this time, Earl met a successful businessman by the name of Lloyd Conant, and together they began an electronic publishing company that eventually grew to become a multimillion-dollar giant in the self-improvement field. They also developed a syndicated, five-minute, daily radio program, *Our Changing World*, which became the longest-running, most widely syndicated show in radio. Nightingale-Conant Corporation has gone on to publish the audiocassette programs of such well-known authors as Tom Peters, Harvey Mackay, Napoleon Hill, Leo Buscaglia, Denis Waitley, Roger Dawson, Wayne Dyer, Brian Tracy, Tony Robbins, and others too numerous to mention—all leaders in personal and professional development.

When Earl Nightingale died on March 28, 1989, Paul Harvey broke the news to the country on his radio program with the words, "The sonorous voice of the nightingale was stilled." While he was alive, Earl had found an answer to the question that had inspired him as a youth. He was able to reach valuable goals and, in turn, leave a lasting legacy for others. He had created a life that defines what it means to be "The Essence of Success." In the words of his good friend and commercial announcer Steve King, "Earl Nightingale never let a day go by that he didn't learn something new and, in turn, to pass it on to others. It was his consuming passion."